A Parent's Guide to Getting Kids Out of the Family Bed

A 21-Day Program

LAWRENCE E. SHAPIRO, PH.D.

Instant Help Books
A Division of New Harbinger Publications, Inc.

Publisher's Note

This publication is designed to provide accurate and authoritative information in regard to the subject matter covered. It is sold with the understanding that the publisher is not engaged in rendering psychological, financial, legal, or other professional services. If expert assistance or counseling is needed, the services of a competent professional should be sought.

Distributed in Canada by Raincoast Books

Copyright © 2008 by Lawrence E. Shapiro
        Instant Help Books
        A Division of New Harbinger Publications, Inc.
        5674 Shattuck Avenue
        Oakland, CA 94609
        www.newharbinger.com

Cover design by Amy Shoup

Cover photo is a model used for illustrative purposes only.

Printed in the United States of America

Library of Congress Cataloging-in-Publication Data

Shapiro, Lawrence E.
  A parent's guide to getting kids out of the family bed : a twenty-one day program / Lawrence E. Shapiro.
     p. cm.
  ISBN-13: 978-1-57224-608-9 (pbk. : alk. paper)
  ISBN-10: 1-57224-608-1 (pbk. : alk. paper) 1. Co-sleeping. 2. Infants--Sleep. I. Title.
  GT3000.5.C67S53 2008
  649'.122--dc22

               2008016266

10   09   08

10   9   8   7   6   5   4   3   2   1

First printing

Contents

Introduction

Are you reading this sentence with your eyes at half-mast? Cosleeping can be an exhausting enterprise for parents; one mother of a seven-year-old described sleeping in the bed with her daughter as the equivalent of sleeping inside a washing machine. But whether you chose cosleeping or cosleeping chose you, there is a way to end it without the battles and tears you might expect. In twenty-one days, you and your child can be enjoying a more restful night's sleep.

Since you're reading this book, I assume that you're ready to stop sleeping in the same bed as your child. If your child is over eighteen months of age, I think that this is a good choice. As a child psychologist, and as a father, I believe that sleeping with a child under eighteen months is a personal choice that may benefit parents as well as children. You can argue the pros and cons of cosleeping with young children, just like you can argue the benefits of breastfeeding or bottle feeding, but ultimately every family's decision must be made with very real, practical considerations in mind, and there is no right or wrong decision. In spite of what some people may claim, there is no hard evidence to say that sleeping with your child is any better or worse than sleeping in separate beds or in different rooms.

There are varied reasons why parents choose cosleeping. Most who do choose it believe that it fosters a bond between them and their infants. These parents often subscribe to a popular parenting style called attachment parenting, which contends that cosleeping supports children's development of empathy and emotional connectedness, potentially preventing a variety of emotional and behavioral problems. Cosleeping is only one aspect of attachment parenting, which promotes all kinds of closeness between parents and their children, including breastfeeding and baby wearing. Advocates of attachment parenting are quick to point out that this method of child rearing does not rely so much on specific behaviors, but rather on a state of mind that supports nurturing and closeness in the family. It is worth noting that attachment parenting doesn't necessarily advocate that young children sleep in the same bed with their parents, but rather that they sleep close to their parents—in the same room. And while many pediatricians also advise having children under a year of age sleep in the same room as their parents as a way to reduce the occurrence of sudden infant death syndrome (SIDS), they usually caution parents against cosleeping with infants to avoid the possibility of rolling over on them or having them suffocate in the bedding.

A second group of parents sleep with their children as a matter of convenience. These parents lead hectic lives and find that nighttime is a good time to enjoy the physical closeness of their children. These parents often say that they go to bed early anyway because they are so tired, and they find the time spent cuddling before sleep is just the right way to end a day. They also say that cosleeping avoids bedtime battles, which would add too much stress to the end of the day.

A third group of parents find themselves sleeping with their children without any real thought or intention. Some of these parents say that their cosleeping began with a child's illness, and the child simply never went back to her own bed. Others say their cosleeping began with a period of nightmares or nighttime fears that disappeared in the family bed. Since no parents want to see their child anxious or afraid, sleeping in the family bed just seems easier than forcing a child to face his fears.

Finally, there is a group of parents that cosleep so that they won't be alone. Typically this happens after a divorce or after a death in the family. In these cases, the child may be perfectly happy sleeping by himself, but the parent needs solace, and there are few things in life that calm our worries or allay our grief more then a sleeping child.

Of these four reasons, only the first is truly in the best interest of your child. Sleeping with your child because you haven't spent time with him during the day is not a trade-off that benefits him. Avoiding bedtime battles because you're too tired or stressed is ignoring your parental responsibility; you can't raise happy, healthy, and caring children by just giving in to their demands. Cosleeping with your child when she is scared or has nightmares is fine for a night, but you have to teach her to face her fears. And sleeping with your child for your own emotional needs, while often understandable, does neither of you a service.

The Benefits of Children Sleeping in Their Own Beds

There are three basic reasons why I believe that cosleeping past the age of eighteen months is not in the best interests of the family.

1. Cosleeping for the wrong reasons, as described earlier, detracts from your parenting power as well as your ability to have a close relationship with your spouse. Good parenting is certainly about nurturing and loving, but these are primarily daytime activities. Good parenting is also about setting rules, limits, and boundaries, and bedtime is one of the most important times to do this.

2. You and your child need a good night's sleep. Sleep is as vital to your health as food and exercise. Anything that disrupts this regenerative process, even if it's your sweet, adoring child, must be addressed. You can't be a good parent, employee, or spouse if you're not getting enough sleep.

3. Teaching your child to sleep in her own bed reinforces her sense of autonomy and self-reliance. As painful as it can sometimes be, raising children is a process of letting go. From the moment of birth, but particularly after eighteen months,

your job is to guide your child's journey toward becoming an independent and resourceful person. Keeping an older child in your bed—to avoid struggles, anxieties, or for your own reasons—denies her the opportunity to develop the emotional skills she needs to meet life's challenges.

The 21-Day Program

This 21-day program for getting your child out of the family bed works on two levels: emotional and behavioral. Each day presents a new parenting skill that will contribute to your child's emotional growth and your own. The related activities are based on tenets of family therapy, child development research, and a relatively new field of psychology: emotional intelligence. Emotional-intelligence theory helps us understand emotional development by defining specific skills that people have to learn, such as emotional communication, emotional management, getting along with others, and having a positive attitude. Some children naturally have a high degree of emotional-intelligence skills, and others need a little boost. This is true of adults, too. For example, some parents explain that they are having a hard time getting their children out of the family bed because they themselves are too anxious or find it too hard to say no. This program is designed to give you and your child the tools needed to make this transition easier. For ease of reading, both genders have been used in examples throughout the book.

The behavioral program, explained below, is based on widely accepted principles of positive reinforcement. It's simple: When your child sleeps in his own bed, he gets a reward. When he sleeps in your bed, he doesn't.

The Emotional Program

The activities that you will do each day are divided into three sections, one for each week of the program.

Week 1: During this week, you'll think about the reasons that your child is still in your bed, and you'll prepare yourself for this important family transition. You and your spouse will commit to this decision and also learn how ending the habit of cosleeping will reinforce an overall positive parenting style.

Week 2: During this week, you and your family will focus on the lifelong benefits of healthy sleep habits. You'll learn the importance of bedtime rituals, and how to teach kids to self-calm when they are anxious or upset. You will learn to handle common problems—like nightmares and separation anxiety—that can lead to cosleeping.

Week 3: In the last week of the program, you'll foster your child's emotional development by encouraging age-appropriate independence and resiliency. You will also learn how you can nurture a positive relationship with your child that will last a lifetime.

The Behavioral Program

The behavioral program presented in this book is based on one of the most powerful techniques in psychology—positive reinforcement. Simply put, positive reinforcement makes a behavior (like getting your child to sleep in his bed) more likely to occur by consistently rewarding that behavior. There are two types of rewards that work with children: intangible rewards (like praise and affection) and tangible rewards (like certificates, stickers, treats, and special privileges). Over the course of the 21 days, we'll use both.

Every day for 21 days, your child will get praise and attention for staying in her bed. You can punctuate your praise with hugs, kisses, tickles, pats, and other signs of affection. You'll make at least four specific positive comments that convey your pleasure at her success, as well as in her achievement of acting like an older child. It also helps to include comments about how sleeping in her own bed can bring future benefits. Some examples are:

- I'm so proud of you!
- That was really grown up of you to stay in your own bed!
- You're just like all the big kids!
- It's great that you slept by yourself. Now you can have a sleepover sometime soon.
- You were as quiet as a mouse last night! You didn't wake Mommy and Daddy even once.

The tangible rewards will vary, depending on your child's age.

- For children eighteen to twenty-four months, there is a different reward certificate for each day. Display it in your child's room or in a prominent place in the home.
- For children twenty-four to thirty-six months, you'll use the same reward certificate, but have your child color it in. You may even want to make several copies for her to color in during the day.

- For children from four to six years old, the Happy-Face chart in Appendix A will be most appropriate, although your child may like a daily reward certificate too. Each time your older child sleeps in his own bed, have him color in a happy face on the chart and give him a special reward from a grab bag, which can contain stickers, pencils, and items similar to what you would put in a party bag. You can also put in slips of paper with extra privileges written on them, like "You get a special dessert for dinner," "You get extra time on the computer," or "You get to rent a movie." The surprise is as important as the reward, so don't let your child see what is in the bag! Have him close his eyes when he chooses his reward.

No matter what your child's age, always remember to heap on the praise when your child sleeps in her own bed!

At the End of the 21-Day Program

At the end of the 21 days, your child will be sleeping in his own bed. You must make this clear to him and commit yourself to it, too. Your spouse must also agree that after 21 days, there is no turning back.

The positive-reinforcement program is designed to give your child a sense of control over his behavior. He will learn that he gets all kinds of rewards for making a good choice.

Your child gets rewarded for staying in his own bed from the very first day, and that might be the last time you have an argument about his sleeping arrangements. But even if he quickly begins to sleep in his own bed, completing the program can help you become a more consistent parent and help your child become more responsible and self-reliant.

On the other hand, your child may continue to argue and fuss about sleeping by himself, and he may say he doesn't care about the certificates or rewards. Again, continue the 21-day program anyway, even if he continues to sleep in your bed and doesn't get any rewards. The activities that you do each day will still be important.

You will have to remind your child that he will absolutely, definitely, positively, without a doubt be sleeping in his own bed on Day 22 and from then on, whether he gets rewards or not. So he might as well as get the rewards!

If Your Child Doesn't Respond to the
Positive Behavior Program

This is the hard part. For 21 days, you will be taking a reasoned, psychologically correct approach to getting your child out of your bed. If you follow it with resolve, it should work with about 85 percent of children. If you follow it halfheartedly, that number will drop to 50 percent or less.

And there will always be some children who resist even the best-laid parenting plans. These children, sometimes referred to as strong willed and spirited, other times referred to as oppositional and willful, are just more difficult to manage. You probably already know if your child fits this description but if you are unsure, take the test in Appendix B.

If your child falls into the group of children who don't sleep in their beds after 21 days, you have several choices:

- Lock your bedroom door so that your child can't come in.
- Put a baby gate in front of your child's bedroom door, if you think your younger child may leave her room. Use a baby monitor to keep an eye on her.
- Take a parenting course on handling children with behavior problems.
- Consult a parenting expert by phone. You will find many parent consultants by searching the Internet, but make sure you take the time to check their references and credentials.
- Hire a parenting coach to come to your home.

Any of these alternatives will help, and two-thirds of children who don't respond to the 21-day program will respond to the first two approaches.

Success depends on your resolve to see this through. If you're serious about getting your strong-willed child out of your bed, then sign the pledge on the next page, and ask your spouse to sign, too. Ask two family members or friends to witness your pledge. Signing this pledge is a promise to yourself, and having witnesses sign it is a public acknowledgment of your intentions. Researchers tell us that by signing this type of pledge you will get increase the power of your commitment by up to 40 percent.

I/we _____,
        (your name and name of your spouse)

agree that _____
              (name of your child)

will not sleep in my/our bed after _____, no matter what!
                                          (date)

Signed:

_____

_____

Witnessed:

_____

_____

When Nothing Seems to Work

As mentioned earlier, 85 percent of children should respond to the 21-day program described in this book. Fifteen percent will still be sleeping in the parents' bed after 21 days, but a simple commitment to lock your door or put up a physical barrier will do the trick for another 10 percent of children. That leaves 5 percent of children who will find a way to get around their parents' resolve. I can't predict exactly what these kids will do, but I have known children who pound on the walls all night, who destroy things in their rooms, and who become much more difficult in their daytime behavior in order to establish their control over their families. If your child falls into this 5 percent, you need to seek the help of a professional therapist, preferably a psychologist with experience in working with oppositional children. Your child's oppositional personality and limit-testing behavior will not go away, and you do him and the rest of your family a disservice if you ignore it.

Week 1:
Preparing Yourself and Your Family

There are probably many reasons why you have waited this long to get your child out of the family bed. Maybe you didn't think she was ready for this transition. Maybe you didn't think you were ready. Many parents simply say that they are too tired to face the stress that goes along with a major transition.

By choosing this book, you have signaled your decision that now is the time. Week 1 will lay the groundwork for this change and hopefully reduce the stress of getting your child to sleep in his own bed.

Read through all the activities before you begin, and if any of them don't apply to your situation, simply skip over them.

When you begin the program, say to your child something like:

> "It's time to sleep in your own bed. I know that you like sleeping with me and Daddy, but it really is hard to get a good night's sleep with you in our bed. You need to sleep in your own bed because you will sleep better, and you will have privacy too.

> "We're going to start a fun program that will help you get used to staying in your own bed. It will last three weeks [you can show a calendar to your child to demonstrate this], and then you will be sleeping in your own bed every night. Every night that you sleep in your own bed, you will get a special reward or treat. I can't tell you what that reward will be; you'll just have to see for yourself."

If at all possible, do the activities with your spouse, expressing your thoughts and feelings as you go along. If you share custody, let your former spouse know that you're embarking on an important transition in your child's life, and encourage his or her commitment to the same process. Any other caregiver who has your child overnight in the next few weeks will need to know your plans in advance. As in all aspects of raising children, the more you keep things consistent in your child's life, the easier it will be for your child.

The 21-day program is a positive discipline program that rewards your child for sleeping in his bed and also teaches him why this is important. The intention of the program is to motivate your child to want to sleep by himself rather than to force a confrontation. I assume that confronting your child about sleeping in his own bed did not work in the past. Most parents find that this positive approach is much easier on the entire family; *however, don't forget that you must be firm in giving your child the message that he will be sleeping in his own bed by the end of the program.*

> Today you'll think about the importance of getting a good night's sleep for both you and your child.

Does This Sound Like Your Family?

Randi was always a go-getter, even as a child. She was the most ambitious of her siblings, the first to join clubs at school, the first to complete her homework early, the first to ... well, everything. She was a Type A personality by the time she was ten.

Randi continued her headlong pursuit of challenges and her need to be active into her teens. She always studied hard, staying up late every night to get the grades and SAT scores that could admit her into her choice of Ivy League schools.

Her pace did not slacken when she finished college and then law school. She spent her twenties writing briefs and pulling all-nighters to prepare for cases and was well on her way to becoming a partner in her firm before she was thirty.

At thirty-three, she had her first child, David. She worked until the last day of pregnancy and refused to take more than three months of maternity leave. When David, as a toddler, started climbing into the family bed, her husband protested but Randi insisted David be allowed to stay, committed to whatever seemed best for their son.

Her sleep was constantly interrupted, but she fueled herself with coffee, welcomed the nanny, and trudged to her office every morning at eight, no matter what. She ignored her mental fogginess and fatigue and continued to run herself ragged.

One afternoon while she was resting her head on her desk, one of the senior partners knocked on her office door. He gently pointed out that her work was suffering and told Randi that if she didn't start taking care of herself, her job would be threatened. Only then did Randi ramp down her work schedule, and talk with her husband about how to get David sleeping in his own bed again.

Many Americans have the same attitude as Randi: that sleep is a luxury. The ever-increasing consumption of triple-shot lattes speaks to more than just a love of good coffee. We are a nation that can't stay awake because we just don't get enough sleep.

A good night's sleep—seven to eight hours a night for most adults—is a necessity, not a luxury. We are all familiar with the effects of going without sleep: We become irritable and we struggle to be attentive and productive. Lack of sleep also lowers our serotonin levels, and low serotonin levels are associated with a variety of mental health problems that include depression, eating disorders, obsessive-compulsive disorder, and behavior problems.

Chronic lack of sleep can also be a serious health hazard. Heart disease, obesity, and diabetes are just a few of the serious problems that can result from a chronic lack of sleep. Sleep deprivation causes memory loss, a decrease in reaction time, and a general decline in health. Researchers tell us that a chronic lack of sleep can also take years off our lives.

If this gloomy picture isn't enough to get you committed to a good night's sleep, consider the lessons you are teaching your children by ignoring your own need for sleep. Children learn what they see, and when you ignore your basic health needs, you are teaching your children to do the same.

Becoming the Parent You Want to Be

Knowing the facts about sleep and using what you know to change your behavior are two different things. Read the following facts, and put a check mark next to each item that you already know but have ignored.

Regularly getting a good night's sleep can help to:

☐ Keep your heart healthy
Getting between seven and nine hours of sleep at night can help you avoid heart disease.

☐ Protect against cancer
Melatonin, a hormone that appears to suppress the growth of tumors and protects

against cancer, is higher in people who get adequate sleep. Keeping your bedroom dark at night will increase the benefits of melatonin.

☐ Reduce stress
When you don't get enough sleep, your body goes into a state of distress, which can cause an increase in blood pressure and the production of stress hormones. Higher levels of these hormones make it harder to sleep, possibly resulting in a cycle of insomnia.

☐ Reduce inflammation
Those same pesky stress hormones increase inflammation, creating higher risk for heart-related problems, diabetes, and cancer. Inflammation can also cause visible signs of aging, which is part of the reason people who get enough sleep look more youthful.

☐ Keep you more alert
There's no better way to increase your energy and be your best self all through the day. Getting a good night's sleep also improves memory. Some researchers believe that dreaming helps you process information and build connections between memories, sensory data, emotions, and events.

☐ Maintain a healthy weight
Lack of sleep affects hormone balance and appetite and has been associated with obesity in children and adults.

☐ Reduce depression
Those who sleep well are more likely to have higher serotonin levels.

Are you getting enough precious sleep? You know that it's nearly impossible to be an effective parent on little to no sleep. Make a commitment now, for the sake of yourself and your family, to move forward in the process.

It's a Fact

Children find it easiest to change their behavior when you acknowledge their feelings and go on to state your expectations in a positive way. You could say to your five-year-old: "I know it'll be hard for you to stay in your own bed tonight, and you might feel scared or lonely. But I know that you will do your best."

Did you explain the 21-day program to your child?

☐ Yes   ☐ No

Write down how your child reacted.

_____

_____

_____

_____

Was your nighttime ritual different than it usually is? _____

If your child came into your bed, what time was it? _____

Is this a different time than usual? _____

What did you do?

_____

_____

What did you say?

_____

_____

What happened next?

_____

_____

You did it!

Today you'll think about the things that have kept you from getting your child out of your bed.

Does This Sound Like Your Family?

Gail and Peter are typical modern parents: both busy and on the go, with little downtime. Even though Gail made a conscious decision to give up her successful career as a journalist to be a stay-at-home mom, she misses her job at the newspaper. Samantha, age twenty-eight months, is her pride and joy, but her "terrible twos" have kept Gail from her home office, where she hopes to begin a freelance career. Every time she sits down to write, Samantha seems to wake up and need attention.

Gail and Peter read every book there is on parenting, often check out popular website forums about raising kids, and constantly exchange ideas with other parents of young children. This is why they chose to cosleep when Samantha was an infant—they were sure it was best for her.

Unlike Peter, Gail was a light sleeper, and Samantha's kicking and constant movement kept her awake. When Samantha was eleven months old, Peter pointed out that it had been ages since Gail had gotten a decent night of sleep. He suggested that they try to put Samantha in her crib.

Because they were embarrassed to tell any of their friends that they were "failures" at cosleeping, they didn't bother to consult anyone with older children. Instead, they plunged in, simply putting Samantha in her room at her usual bedtime. After about five minutes of high-pitched wailing, Gail couldn't take it anymore, so she rushed in and swept Samantha from her crib. She told herself that she'd have more willpower the next night.

On night two, Peter told Gail to plug her ears or go into the living room to keep out of hearing distance. This time, Gail lasted seven minutes. When she returned to the family bed with a calmed Samantha in her arms, she looked at her husband and said, "I just can't do this. Not now." She was just too guilty and too tired to make the transition.

Day 2

You likely have your own story of trying and failing to get your child out of your bed. But guess what? Every parent feels like a failure at some time. It just goes with the territory. There is no such thing as a perfect parent, but we should all strive to be "good enough" parents. Good-enough parents usually do the right thing at the right time, but sometimes they make mistakes. Sometimes they make the same mistake over and over. Sometimes they do things that are less than ideal but they rationalize that their love for the child will compensate for their imperfections.

Whatever the reasons that your child is sleeping in your bed, whatever past mistakes you have made, it is time to let that go.

Before beginning a program to get your child out of the family bed, it's essential to get to the heart of any ambivalence that you or your spouse may have about this change in your family's life. The following exercise will help you to figure out where you stand.

Becoming the Parent You Want to Be

In the space below, honestly reflect on why your child is still sleeping in your bed. If you're concerned about your spouse reading your thoughts, you can use a separate notebook or journal that is private. Just write what you're thinking without editing yourself or being self-critical; try to let your thoughts flow without holding back.

This type of free association works best when it's timed, so set an alarm for ten minutes, then put your pen to paper and keep it moving.

Being completely frank with yourself about a topic as emotional as cosleeping is a key step in the process of getting your child out of the family bed. If you have any feelings of shame, ambivalence, anger, fear, or sadness associated with the experience, that's perfectly normal.

What Has Held Me Back

It's a Fact

Your child's most important reward is your praise and approval. If your child succeeds in staying in her own bed, make a big deal out of this accomplishment. But even if your child doesn't succeed, look for some small improvement to praise. Can't think of anything about the nighttime behavior to praise? Then praise some other aspect of her behavior that shows independence and responsibility.

Did your child get a Happy Face or other reward for sleeping in his or her own bed?

_____

Write down how your child reacted.

_____

_____

_____

_____

Was your nighttime ritual different than it usually is? _____

If your child came into your bed, what time was it? _____

Is this a different time than usual? _____

What did you do?

_____

_____

What did you say?

_____

_____

Is there anything that you will do differently tonight?

_____

_____

Wow—you're the best!

Day 3

Good Reasons to Change Your Sleeping Situation

> Today you'll think about the positive benefits of getting your child out of the family bed.

Does This Sound Like Your Family?

Jen was the single mother of two-year-old Jason. When her marriage broke up right after she gave birth, Jen was devastated and in need of affection. It seemed natural to bring her baby into her bed; after all, he was warm and cuddly, and it certainly made breastfeeding much easier. She frequently said, "Jason's the only man I need in my life."

After several months, some of Jen's friends became concerned that she was using her son to take the place of an adult relationship. They encouraged her to look for potential partners online, but in her heart, Jen was afraid that no one would want the mother of a young child, with all the inherent baggage. She looked at profiles, but never e-mailed anyone and ignored the men who were interested in her.

No matter how well she knew that it was the right thing, Jen couldn't bring herself to place her son in his room at night. It's not like Jason was a fussy child; in fact he was easygoing and did not really have a problem separating from Jen at nursery school or when he was dropped off at his grandma's house. Jen told herself that it was just not the right time for Jason to sleep alone. She thought, "I'll know when it's the right time, and then I'll do it." But she stopped talking about her cosleeping with her friends and family. When Jason was three, he was still sleeping in his mother's bed.

When is the best time to end cosleeping? From a developmental perspective, it is when your child is between eighteen and twenty-four months old. Whether your child is in your actual bed or in a crib in your room, cosleeping certainly supports a close bond between you. This bond, which is also formed by unconditional love, constant hugs and caresses, and millions of kisses, is the most important part of your job in parenting your young baby. But while your physical affection for your child will continue for many years and your unconditional love will never end, there is another developmental task for you and your child that begins at around a year and a half, and that is fostering autonomy—your child's sense of himself.

When your child learns to sleep by himself, he will be a different person, someone who doesn't need to be with Mommy and Daddy all the time. That may seem like a significant change for parents who have enjoyed the indescribable closeness one can have with an infant—and it is. But parenting is both about loving and letting go. This is a lesson you will learn again and again.

Becoming the Parent You Want to Be

The more you look at the benefits of getting your child to sleep in her own bed, the easier it will be. The following are the most commonly listed benefits of getting children out of the family bed. Rate each one from 1 to 7, with 1 = Not really important to me and 7 = Very important to me.

_____ I will be able to get a good night's sleep.

_____ My spouse and I can have a better sexual relationship.

_____ I will stop feeling guilty about having my child in my bed.

_____ My child will be able to have sleepovers.

_____ My family and friends will leave me alone about this issue.

_____ I can go to bed later.

_____ I can get up at a different time than my child does.

Can you think of any other benefits? List them here and rate them.

_____

_____

_____

It's a Fact

Focusing on the positive benefits of a situation really does make a difference in your behavior. Psychologists have found again and again that changing your thoughts is a key ingredient in changing how you act.

Did your child get a Happy Face or other reward for sleeping in his or her own bed?

_____

Write down how your child reacted.

_____

_____

_____

_____

Was your nighttime ritual different than it usually is? _____

If your child came into your bed, what time was it? _____

Is this a different time than usual? _____

What did you do?

_____

_____

What did you say?

_____

_____

Is there anything that you will do differently tonight?

_____

_____

You are amazing!

Today you will learn about your parenting style, and how it affects your decision to get your child out of the family bed.

Does This Sound Like Your Family?

Heather had been a strong-willed child since the time she was an infant. She was a finicky eater and fussed at any change in her routine. She threw tantrums when she didn't get her way, which did not happen too often. When Heather wanted something, her parents, Tom and Nora, had a difficult time saying no. She wasn't required to eat what her parents were eating and every night had a special dinner prepared for her, which she usually refused. Most nights she ate just yogurt. Although their house was large, it always seemed crowded because it was filled to the brim with Heather's toys. No matter what time of day it was, when Heather wanted to play, Nora felt compelled to play with her. She might have a backache or headache, be in the middle of folding laundry, or just be plain tuckered out. Still, Heather was never just told no.

Day 4

Psychologists have been researching what it takes to make a good parent for decades, and they have concluded that there are three general types of parenting styles:

- *Authoritarian parents* value obedience above all else. They command their children about what to do and what not to do, and their rules are unbending. Misbehavior is strictly punished. Children with authoritarian parents are typically well behaved when they are young, but they may rebel as teens.

- *Permissive parents* let their children take the lead. They take a hands-off approach to discipline and believe that their children will eventually find their way. Rules may be stated and randomly enforced, but permissive parents are quick to give children another chance. Many children raised this way continually test their parents' limits. Because they are used to getting their way, they may have difficulty adjusting to the give-and-take of friendships.

- *Authoritative parents* have clear rules and limits, and they tell their children the reasons behind what they do. Teaching children to be responsible is a high priority in the family, and children are given lots of practice making choices and living with the consequences of those choices. Children raised in this type of family tend to have an easier time in school and later in work.

As you might have guessed, psychologists assert that authoritative parents raise children who have the fewest problems and the most success in their lives. Studies suggest that permissive parenting can be just as detrimental to a child's development as authoritarian parenting, and it should come as no surprise that permissive parents are the ones most likely to have problems getting children to sleep in their own beds.

Becoming the Parent You Want to Be

Many parents don't see that they are too permissive. They love their child above all else, and their foremost desire in life is to feel that their child loves them back. They don't see that setting limits and sometimes displeasing their child is a part of being a loving parent.

Are you a permissive parent? Take the following test and find out. A score of 50 or higher means that you should work on learning to set limits for your child.

Rate the following statements from 1 to 7, with 1 = never and 7 = always.

_____ Your child's bedtime changes every night.

_____ Your child decides what he or she will have for dinner.

_____ You pick up after your child.

_____ Your child talks back and you don't say anything to stop this behavior.

_____ You buy your child something every time you go shopping together.

_____ Your child watches TV whenever he or she wants to.

_____ Your child eats "junk" food whenever he or she wants to.

_____ You feel you have to reward your child for doing things he or she doesn't like, such as doing errands with you.

_____ You feel that you have to be your child's playmate when he or she is bored.

_____ You plan your weekends and free time exclusively around your child's interests.

Day 4

If you want to be an authoritative parent, here are four things you can try. Try each and then write your thoughts and observations on the lines provided.

1. Write your household rules on a piece of paper and post them in a place that your child will see frequently. Even if your child does not read yet, writing the rules down will emphasize that they are very important.

   _____

   _____

   _____

   _____

2. Require your child to do chores on a daily basis (see Appendix C for a list of age-appropriate chores).

   _____

   _____

   _____

   _____

3. Have a family meeting once a week. Use the meeting to talk about problems that have occurred during the week. Let children know that they have an important voice in the family but that you are still in charge of major decisions.

    _____

    _____

    _____

    _____

4. Review your child's time in front of the TV or computer. Children should not spend more than an hour and a half a day in front of a screen. If your child spends more time watching TV or playing video games, use a timer to limit these sedentary activities.

    _____

    _____

    _____

    _____

Changing your parenting style does not happen overnight, so be patient and, above all, be consistent.

It's a Fact

Being strict does not mean being harsh. Strict parents set clear rules and limits and do not waver from them. Research tells us that parents who have clear rules and enforce them have children who are happier and more successful.

Did your child get a Happy Face or other reward for sleeping in his or her own bed?

_____

Write down how your child reacted.

_____

_____

_____

_____

Do you think that either you or your spouse is too permissive? _____

Is this part of your problem in getting your child out of the family bed? _____

Who is a good role model for you as a parent? _____

What do you think that person would say or do about your parenting style?

_____

_____

_____

Can you ask that person for help or advice?

_____

_____

_____

You are fantastic!

Today you'll think about ways to teach your child good behavior without resorting to frequent punishment.

Does This Sound Like Your Family?

David and Wendy had different opinions about how to discipline Ethan, their rambunctious four-year-old. David believed that sending Ethan to his room or swatting him on the behind was the best way to deal with misbehavior, but Wendy thought that she should reason with Ethan when he was breaking a rule—which was often.

Ethan would forget to pick up his toys and to wash his hands before a meal. He would brush his teeth only if one of his parents were standing over him. Otherwise, he would squirt the toothpaste on the counter and brush it. In David's opinion, his son was too wild and irresponsible, even for a four-year-old. Wendy thought that Ethan was just going through a stage and would soon learn to follow the household rules.

Wendy hated to see her husband lose his temper with Ethan and often found herself hovering over him when David was around so that Ethan would behave appropriately.

When Wendy got a call from Ethan's preschool teacher, she realized that neither she nor her husband had the right answers when it came to his behavior. Ethan's teacher said that he rarely sat still and didn't seem to care about the classroom rules. The other kids were complaining that Ethan wouldn't share the toys or wait his turn.

Many parents have problems disciplining their children and, like David and Wendy, do not have a clear strategy to teach them how to behave. Often parents don't think about how they discipline until someone outside the immediate family comments on a child's behavior. The comments most frequently come from a teacher, a grandparent, or another close relative.

Punishment is not the best way to teach children good behavior. As you will see in Day 6, there are times when effective punishment is the only way to stop misbehavior, but stopping children from misbehaving and teaching them good behavior are two different things. Unfortunately, reasoning does not help either, particularly with a young child. If it did, life as a parent would be much easier. Psychologists often point out to parents that children don't have the cognitive development to understand why certain behaviors are wrong and others are right, and that rational arguments go only so far even with adults. If we all acted reasonably and responded to clear logic, none of us would smoke, overeat, or lose our tempers, but that just isn't the way the human mind works.

Positive discipline, which is what I recommend to parents 90 percent of the time, is different from punishment or reasoning. It is a method of teaching children good behavior. The philosophy of positive discipline is simple: When you teach children about how to be good and the importance of being good, they won't misbehave, and they won't need the kind of punishments—scolding, time-out, loss of privileges—that many children experience on a daily basis.

When you teach your child the skills that define good behavior—cooperativeness, empathy, emotional communication, and so on—you will find that it is hardly necessary to punish her. You will also find it much easier to deal with the task of getting her out of the family bed.

Becoming the Parent You Want to Be

There are many ways to teach children good behavior. First and foremost is to be a good role model. Talk about your feelings and respect the feelings of others. When you are angry, count to ten and take several calming breaths before you say or do anything. If you want your child to be neat, be organized yourself. If you want your child to develop good health habits, provide a good example.

The second most important thing you can do is to take ten minutes a day to teach children about good values and good behavior. Just ten minutes a day can make a world of difference. There are many ways to teach children about good behavior, and one technique I often recommend to parents is playing cooperative games.

Cooperative games focus children (and parents) on the need to work together. Imagine if your child thought, "I'll cooperate because it's good for the whole family," rather than, "I'll do what I want because it's good for me." Certainly many parenting tasks would be easier, including getting children out of the family bed.

Unlike typical games that children play, where one person is the winner and everyone else loses, in a cooperative game everyone wins—or everyone loses if the players don't cooperate.

One fun game that I often "prescribe" is called the Cooperative-Robot Game. In this game, the child stands between his parents and holds each one's hand. The family acts as a robot—a cooperative robot—with the goal of helping out around the house. The child is the "brain" and the parents each use their free hand.

Now the fun begins. Try joining hands with your child and spouse and then doing a simple task, like making a peanut-butter sandwich. It's not as easy as you might think! But the real object of the game is to learn to cooperate without bickering or blaming, and to have fun at the same time. Now try other tasks, like cleaning up toys from the floor, vacuuming the carpet, or scooping out three bowls of ice cream.

There are many ways you can teach children about good behavior and good values rather than waiting to punish them when they misbehave. Try reading your child books about values, using popular series like the Berenstain Bears. Emphasize the importance of being a helpful and caring person by having children join you in charitable or community-service activities. And don't forget to tell children how their behavior affects others (including you). This promotes empathy and helps children understand the give-and-take of relationships.

It's a Fact

Nearly 50 percent of children who see a counselor are referred because of a behavior problem. The window of opportunity for helping children with behavior problems is ages three to eight, when they are most sensitive to adult expectations and most anxious to please adults.

Did your child get a Happy Face or other reward for sleeping in his or her own bed?

_____

Write down how your child reacted.

_____

_____

_____

_____

How did you sleep last night? _____

Did you think about how you can be proactive in teaching your child good behavior?

_____

What are other things you can do to promote good behavior?

_____

_____

_____

Are you a good role model for children? What might you do differently?

_____

_____

_____

_____

Tremendously stupendous!

What to Do When Misbehavior Occurs

Today you'll evaluate how you react when your child misbehaves or breaks a rule, and you'll look at whether your style of discipline is working.

Does This Sound Like Your Family?

Risa, a single mother of two children, often complained about her problems in disciplining Brooke, her rather trying five-year-old. "Brooke is always testing me," Risa told the school counselor. "If I say it's time to get ready for school in the morning, she says, 'No, it's not. I need more time.' If I ask her to eat her vegetables, she stops eating any of her dinner. If I tell her that she has to sleep in her own bed, she throws a fit, and by the end of the day, I'm too exhausted to punish her for being so obstinate. Just yesterday, she was sent to her room five times. And every time I tell her to go to her room, there's a struggle. I have no idea of what to do to make life easier between us."

The first thing Risa needs to do is to stop sending Brooke to her room. Why? Because it doesn't work! When parents tell me, "I yell at my child all the time, and he still doesn't listen" or "I get so mad I spank my child, and it has no effect," I invariably say, "Stop doing those things. They obviously don't work, or you wouldn't have to do them again and again." Many parents seem to miss this obvious point: if their discipline style worked, their children would stop misbehaving.

When it comes to punishing children who misbehave, there are two techniques I recommend: putting children in time-out and taking away privileges. Time-out works best with children ages three to six, and after that, taking away privileges is most effective.

Note: A third technique, where children earn points and lose them when they misbehave, is also effective, but since you are already using a Happy Face system in this book to get your child out of the family bed, I don't recommend using this approach for other behaviors. Point systems work best when they address one behavior at a time.

Becoming the Parent You Want to Be

Time-out and loss of privileges work well if you use them correctly, but many parents don't use them consistently or completely. Review the guidelines below if you don't feel that your discipline is working.

How to Use Time-Out

Time-out works with most children ages three to six if you can remember the 6:60 rule: don't use more than six words when you put your child in time-out and begin the time-out within sixty seconds of the behavior. This simple reminder takes care of the two problems that most parents have: they talk too much and take too long to give their child the consequence for their behavior. Make sure that the time-out corner does not have anything for the child to play with and that it is away from you and the rest of your family. Have the child stay in the time-out corner for one minute for each year of his age (i.e., a three-year-old is in the corner for three minutes, a four-year-old for four minutes, and so on). The time-out doesn't begin until the child is sitting quietly. Then set the timer and have the child stay seated until it goes off. If the child complains about the time-out or misbehaves again, then it is right back to the corner. Eventually, he will get the message that you are serious.

How to Take Away Privileges

If your child is seven or over, I recommend taking away something she uses for entertainment, like TV, a video game, going on the Internet, or using the phone. Some parents I know punish children by denying them playdates or even going to birthday parties, but I don't agree with this method of punishment. It is important for children to play and to go to birthday parties as part of their social development. You never want to take away something that is important to your child's development.

The litmus test of whether a particular form of discipline works is how often you must use it. You can use the log on the next page to record what happened that caused you to discipline your child, the type of discipline you used, and your child's reaction to the discipline. If your discipline just makes your child angry and his behavior gets worse, try another approach.

Discipline Log

Make an entry for each time you discipline your child. You may be making multiple entries on a given day. In the column on the right, rate your child's reaction from 1 (accepted the discipline well) to 7 (resisted strongly).

	What Happened?	What Did You Do?	How Did Your Child React?
Monday			
Tuesday			
Wednesday			
Thursday			
Friday			
Saturday			
Sunday			

It's a Fact

Ages three to eight is the window of opportunity to teach children good behavior. Children younger than three do not really understand cause-and-effect connections and so may not understand why they are being punished. By eight years of age, children should have learned what their parents and other adults expect of them and should have the self-control to comply with these expectations. If a child continues to be in constant trouble after the age of eight, professional consultation should be considered.

Did your child get a Happy Face or other reward for sleeping in his or her own bed?

_____

Write down how your child reacted.

_____

_____

_____

_____

How did you sleep last night? _____

Do you think that your discipline style affects your ability to get your child out of the family bed?

_____

Do you have a problem being firm and consistent? _____

If the answer is yes, who can help you with your approach to discipline?

_____

_____

_____

_____

Great work!

> Today you'll learn how to work with your spouse to create more consistency in your parenting.

Does This Sound Like Your Family?

Simon and Darcy have two children, a two-year-old girl and a five-year-old boy. Ever since their first child arrived, they've been aware of their vastly different parenting styles. Simon finds it hard to say no to his kids. If they see a toy they like on TV, he goes out and gets it. If they want cookies or a soda, he gives it to them, even if it is just before a meal.

Darcy is the rule maker and enforcer. She thinks that children are too indulged and believes that when they don't get everything they ask for, they learn to appreciate what they have.

Simon agrees with his wife's principles, but it's just hard for him to refuse his kids anything. As a result, when the children climb into their parents' bed some time after midnight each night, they go over to their father's side. He lifts them into the bed, where they remain until morning.

Darcy sees Simon as a weak parent; she resents his saying that he agrees with her and then not following through. She is tired of being seen as the mean parent and she is determined not to be the one to make the rules about the family bed. She doesn't want to fight this battle with her kids alone.

Their parenting differences have put a strain on their marriage, and Darcy has suggested they see a marriage counselor. "I can't go on like this," Darcy told Simon one evening. "Either things change around here, or we just can't live together."

Day 7

Many parents find that they have different ideas about raising their children. Often one takes the lead in making parenting decisions, and the other goes along. As in the case of Darcy and Simon, problems most frequently occur when one spouse voices agreement on basic principles and then does not support those principles.

In this situation, every psychologist will tell you that clear and open communication is the best course of action. Plan a time to talk to your spouse about your children. Be honest and open about the things you did or didn't do. Support each other as parents—it's a difficult and sometimes lonely job.

The best way you can do this is by being an attentive, noncritical listener. When you disagree, be respectful in presenting your opinions and try not to place blame. Usually a compromise can be worked out, but if not, take a break from your conversation and talk about what steps you can take to come to a compromise. Sometimes one parent simply has to go along with the other parent's point of view. Some parents seek the advice of an older family member, religious leader, or counselor. There are all sorts of parenting books, advice columns, blogs, and courses that will help you make good parenting decisions. In the end, the most important thing you can do is be consistent with your children. Children suffer when they get mixed messages from their parents, and whatever problems they have are likely to get worse.

Becoming the Parent You Want to Be

Sit down with your spouse and, together, decide the five most important rules for your household.

1. _____

2. _____

3. _____

4. _____

5. _____

Review the rules and make sure that you both feel you can enforce them. Make any changes you need to.

Now comes the most important part of this activity: agreeing to be consistent. Each of you should read the following contract, then photocopy the page, cut out the contract, and sign it. Keep it someplace in your home where you will both see it frequently but your children will not.

Parental Agreement Contract

After openly and honestly discussing our current situation, _____ and _____ have agreed to value and enforce family rules in the same way. Each of us will commit to this task every day, with love, support, and calmness. Even during moments of stress and tension, we will refrain from yelling, blowing up, or having any sort of meltdown in front our child. If either of us is frustrated, we will find healthy outlets to express our feelings, and we will always find time to talk. We will both set aside extra moments in our busy schedules during this process, making sure to tune in to each other's needs, as well as the needs of our child. We will not blame, malign, or accuse one another of failure, but support each other in raising our precious child.

Signed

_____ and

_____

It's a Fact

Most family therapists agree that the ability of couples to resolve conflicts is a critical part of any relationship and a predictor of satisfaction in the marriage.

Did your child get a Happy Face or other reward for sleeping in his or her own bed?

_____

Write down how your child reacted.

_____

_____

_____

_____

How did you sleep last night? _____

Do you think that you and your spouse do a good job of resolving disagreements?

_____

What would you change?

_____

_____

_____

How much time do you spend talking with your spouse about how you parent?

_____

You make us proud!

Week 2:
The Importance of Sleep

For the next seven days, you'll learn about the importance of sleep. I hope that for the next seven nights you will get a good rest!

As you know, a good night's rest is important to you and your child, and cosleeping is almost always a detriment to a restful sleep. This section will help you develop good sleep habits for you and your child, focusing on preventing the problems that typically land children in their parents' bed long past the time that this is desired.

> Today you'll learn to develop a predictable ritual that will help everyone in the family get a better night's sleep.

Does This Sound Like Your Family?

Pam and Richard have a four-year-old daughter, Daria, and a six-year-old son, Marcus. Both parents work very hard to make ends meet. Richard is a physician assistant in the local hospital, with a schedule that changes every week. Pam is a special-education teacher and also tutors some evenings and weekends.

With their changing work schedules, Pam and Richard find it hard to maintain a consistent routine, so every Sunday they sit down and write out a plan that includes work, household tasks, and the kids' commitments: piano lessons, playdates, soccer games, checkups, and the like.

On Monday mornings, it's off to the races, but although they always keep their written plan in mind, other needs are taken for granted. Dinnertime is usually whenever the kids get hungry, any time between five and seven. Bedtime is also a moving target, depending on what's on TV, whether Marcus has any homework, and whether Daria is in a cooperative mood.

Daria doesn't like to sleep alone; sometimes she'll sleep with her older brother and other times with her parents. She's also been known to sleep on the couch with the TV on, snuggled up next to her father. Somehow, everything seems to work, and yet all the family members seem perpetually tired.

Like many busy parents, Pam and Richard are focused on the calendar and the clock on the wall but pay little attention to the inborn biological clock that is so important to the physical and mental health of each family member.

Each of us has a biological clock that is set according to environmental cues, especially daylight and darkness, and regulated by a number of rhythmic cycles that take about twenty-four hours to complete. These cycles are part of our genetic makeup and regulate all our internal functions, including blood pressure, body temperature, and the secretion of hormones.

If you are a frequent traveler, you know how stressful changing time zones can be. Ever-changing schedules are like that, forcing our biological clocks to constantly reset, but there are many ways to prevent this stress.

- Keep a consistent bedtime routine.
  Most parents start the routine about forty-five minutes before children should be asleep, allowing children time to pick up toys, wash, change into pajamas, and hear a bedtime story. Many children have their own bedtime rituals, like special songs, that may require additional time.

- Keep a consistent waking time.
  Our biological clocks reset in the morning, so this is just as important as a consistent bedtime. Allow enough time so that you are not rushed.

- Don't let your child oversleep on weekends.
  Having sleep hours consistent between weekdays and weekends is the best way to avoid the Monday-morning meltdowns that so many parents encounter.

- Regulate bedroom temperature.
  A cooler temperature is more conducive to sleep.

- Avoid caffeine.
  Soda, chocolate, and energy drinks are all culprits in keeping kids awake. Some families prefer to completely eliminate caffeine from their children's diets; at a minimum, try to avoid caffeine in the evening.

- Keep all electronics out of the bedroom.
  Televisions, phones, and computer games are all sources of stimulation that can interfere with bedtime.

- Have soothing activities before bedtime.
  Come up with a ritual that works for your family, using the hours after dinner as a gradual calming-down time. Avoid scary TV shows and even scary books.

Day 8

Becoming the Parent You Want to Be

The more consistent you are in creating a sleep ritual for your family, the happier and healthier everyone will be.

Describe your child's usual bedtime ritual.

_____

_____

_____

_____

_____

Now describe the ideal bedtime ritual you would like your child to have.

_____

_____

_____

_____

_____

In the left column, write down five things that keep you from adhering to a consistent bedtime ritual. Next to each, in the right column, write a possible way to deal with this interruption.

Interruptions	Solutions

It's a Fact

In a study of nearly one thousand parents, 27 percent reported resistance to going bed as their children's most common sleep-related problem. Other common problems were trouble getting to sleep (11 percent), waking up at night (6 percent), and trouble with morning awakening and daytime tiredness (17 percent).

Did your child get a Happy Face or other reward for sleeping in his or her own bed?

_____

Write down how your child reacted.

_____

_____

_____

_____

How did you sleep last night? _____

What do you need to change about your child's nighttime ritual?

_____

_____

_____

Are you satisfied with your child's bedtime? _____

What do you need to change about your own nighttime ritual to get a better night's sleep?

_____

_____

_____

_____

I like what you did!

> Today you'll learn how to tell bedtime stories that will stimulate your child's natural ability to cope with stress and overcome problems.

Does This Sound Like Your Family?

Bob was the designated storyteller in his house, and he was a very imaginative one at that. He told his three- and five-year-old daughters bedtime stories of sea monsters and pirates, princesses and dragons, and knights to the rescue. Sometimes he even told them futuristic stories about robots that went wild and chased all the people into caves, until a squad of brave little girls tricked the robots into walking into the sea, where they rusted and shut down.

The girls loved Bob's stories and always begged him to tell just one more. But sometimes in the night, both girls would climb into their parents' bed, saying that they had bad dreams about pirates or dragons or robots that killed all the children.

At his wife's insistence, Bob tried switching to gentler bedtime stories, but the girls craved the excitement that their dad would bring to his adventure stories. When they complained about the tame stories, Bob said, "If you keep complaining, I'm going to have to let the tickle monster get hold of you," and he would tickle his daughters until they begged him to stop.

Almost all children like to have bedtime stories told or read to them, often way past the age when they could read the stories themselves. Like Bob, most parents learn that certain stories will keep children up at night, while other stories will relax them so that they can ease into a restful night's sleep. But many parents don't know that stories can also stimulate their children's emotional development and guide them toward independence and self-reliance, which are important goals of this 21-day program.

The state of mind children experience just before they fall asleep is not unlike a hypnotic trance; their minds are very open to suggestions. As children are falling asleep, they seem to absorb messages from the story into their psyches, particularly when those messages have meaning for them. For more than twenty years, psychologists have been prescribing positive bedtime stories as a way to encourage children to face their fears, develop positive attitudes, and cope with a variety of developmental problems. These positive stories give children role models for managing their difficult feelings and overcoming obstacles, both real and perceived. This is an ideal way to give your child messages that will build her confidence and self-esteem.

Day 9

Becoming the Parent You Want to Be

Some parents make up stories as they go, while others prefer to write down their stories and then read them. Either way, with a little practice, you can easily create positive bedtime stories by following this basic formula:

- Create a positive hero.
  Tell stories in which heroes portray positive attitudes toward life and accept their feelings as well as the feelings of others. The hero of your story can be your child, someone like your child, or a fictional character. Young children particularly like stories about animals.

- Emphasize problem solving.
  Introduce a realistic conflict in the story and a realistic solution. Avoid fairy-tale endings where problems are magically solved. The hero should take appropriate steps to solve the problem.

- Teach values.
  Emphasize values that are important to you, and state them in the lesson or moral of your story.

Here is an example of a story told by Nancy, the mother of five-year-old Denise, a shy girl who didn't like new situations or meeting new people.

Once upon a time there were two sisters. One sister liked excitement, and she loved to run, jump, and ride her bike very fast. The other sister was brave in her own way, but she didn't like to do things where she thought she might get hurt.

One day, the whole family went to an amusement park. The first sister wanted to go on all the scary rides, especially the Viper, which was said to be the biggest, scariest roller coaster in the whole world. But the second sister said she was too scared. She was afraid that she might fall off and wanted to go on the merry-go-round instead.

Their parents said that both girls had to go on the rides together, so they definitely had a problem. The second sister said, "I don't want to go on the Viper, because I'm not ready for that. But I will go on the Ferris wheel with you."

(She said this even though she had never gone on a Ferris wheel before.)

"Okay," said the second sister. "That's a compromise. And we can scream and scream if we want. That makes it more fun."

So the two sisters went on the Ferris wheel—ten times! Maybe next time, they would try the roller coaster, too.

The End

The moral: Sometimes if you are afraid of one thing, you can find something not quite so scary to try.

Now try writing a positive story yourself, using this form. Focus this first story on teaching your child the value of cooperating with others.

Title of your story:

_____

Describe your hero.

_____

_____

_____

Give some background information about your hero.

_____

_____

_____

Day 9

Describe your hero's problem or conflict.

_____

_____

_____

Describe a positive realistic solution.

_____

_____

_____

State the moral or lesson of your story.

_____

_____

_____

It's a Fact

One of the reasons stories are so effective in teaching emotional and behavioral skills is that children want to hear them over and over again. Hearing positive stories with similar themes creates a "template" in the mind that children can use to approach real-life problems.

Did your child get a Happy Face or other reward for sleeping in his or her own bed?

_____

Write down how your child reacted.

_____

_____

_____

_____

How did you sleep last night? _____

What story did you like to hear as a child?

_____

Was there a message to this story?

_____

_____

What book did you like as a child?

_____

Was there a message to this book?

_____

_____

You make me so happy!

> Today you'll learn ways to teach your children about the importance of sleep.

Does This Sound Like Your Family?

Joe and Eileen were stuck in a rut with six-year-old Tory. She had been sleeping on her own for several years, but when the family moved into a new home, Tory was back in her parents' bed. She complained of nightmares and said that a ghost lived in her closet.

Tory refused to sleep in her new room, and her parents weren't sure what to do. Eileen had put a lot of work into making Tory's bedroom beautiful and inviting, and she felt like she had to start from square one again.

Joe decided to solve the problem the way his parents had dealt with his nighttime fears. He hid in his daughter's closet at bedtime, and when Eileen went to put Tory to bed, he jumped out and yelled, "Boo!" When Tory began to cry, Joe said, "Look, it's just me. There's nothing to be afraid of." But Tory was inconsolable, and Eileen immediately took her into their bed.

The next day, neither Joe's daughter nor his wife would speak to him. "I'm sorry," Joe said. "I just thought that my being silly would help you see that your fears are silly, too."

Day 10

Bedtime fears, or any fears for that matter, are not always rational. But that doesn't mean that children can't respond to rational and factual information.

Teaching your kids about the importance of sleep is not enough to get them out of your bed, but it will develop the foundation of a lifetime of healthy sleep habits. But first, of course, you must know the facts yourself. Here are the facts behind some common myths.

- There are some children who don't need much sleep.
  In general, children have very specific sleep needs that vary with age. Toddlers need from twelve to fourteen hours (including naps), preschoolers need from eleven to thirteen hours (including naps), and school-age children need from ten to eleven hours of sleep.

- Not getting enough sleep doesn't really hurt kids in the long run.
  Sleep deprivation can have serious consequences for kids, just as it can for adults. A chronic lack of sleep has been associated with obesity, an increase in accidents, a weakening of the immune system, and emotional and behavioral problems.

- It's okay to sleep with the light on.
  When day turns to night, our brains start to produce a chemical called melatonin, which makes us sleepy. Having the lights on confuses the brain and makes it harder to go to sleep.

- Sleeping late on the weekends will make up for lost sleep during the week.
  While sleeping late on the weekends can help make up for a lack of sleep created during the week, it doesn't erase the problems that inadequate sleep causes on a daily basis, including moodiness, irritability, and inattentiveness.

Becoming the Parent You Want to Be

How much time do you spend teaching your children about the importance of a good night's sleep? If you are like most parents, you probably would answer, "No time at all." As important as sleep is to our physical and mental health, most of us just take it for granted, particularly when it comes to kids.

Getting enough sleep is an important reason to move children out of the family bed and into their own rooms. Teaching children the importance of sleep may not help motivate them to see that by themselves, any more than teaching them about the importance of vegetables gets them to try brussels sprouts. But it is still an important part of their health education that you can't ignore.

Fortunately, there are some fun ways to help children learn about sleep. The National Sleep Foundation has a website just for kids: www.sleepforkids.org. This site teaches kids basic sleep facts and comes complete with mazes, word puzzles, and even a printable card game. There are also fact sheets and ideas for parents and teachers.

Here's a game that I recommend to parents to help them get three- to six-year-olds to bed without a fuss. It's called the Bedtime Treasure Hunt Game, and it takes only five to ten minutes.

Day 10

The Bedtime Treasure Hunt Game

Before You Play

You'll need plastic eggs (or other small containers) and small prizes. The prizes might be little balls or toys, stickers, or pieces of paper describing a reward (for example, "We'll read an extra story tonight" or "We can make strawberry waffles for breakfast tomorrow"). Put a prize into a plastic egg and hide it in the child's bedroom.

How to Play

- Tell your child that he can play a fun game if he is ready for bed on time, including getting on his pajamas, washing, brushing his teeth, picking up toys, and so on.
- If your child is ready on time, he gets to hunt for the hidden egg.
- If your child is not ready on time, remove the egg from its hiding place. No prize is given.
- During this 21-day program, play the game once a week on a random basis.

It's a Fact

According to a study conducted by the National Sleep Foundation, the average child gets from 10 to 15 percent less sleep during a twenty-four-hour period than is recommended by sleep experts.

Did your child get a Happy Face or other reward for sleeping in his or her own bed?

_____

Write down how your child reacted.

_____

_____

_____

_____

How did you sleep last night? _____

Is it hard for you to get your child to go to bed? _____

Is there anything you do that makes it harder?

_____

_____

_____

Is there anything someone else does that makes it harder?

_____

_____

_____

_____

I love it when you try so hard!

Today you'll learn about the important roles nutrition and exercise play in your child's sleep.

Does This Sound Like Your Family?

Even though they always feel rushed, neither Stacey nor Jordan would ever skip their half hour on the exercise bike every morning. But when it comes to food, everything is done on the run, including feeding their six-year-old, Sam. Sam has been raised on sugary cereal, high-fructose juices, and high-carbohydrate frozen foods, like pizza and bagels. He hates vegetables, and since his parents want to avoid his fussing, they let it go, just glad to see him eating something.

As soon as he started eating solid foods in his first year, Stacey realized that Sam was a finicky eater. When she went back to work, she told the nanny to let him have what he wanted. When Stacey gets home from work at six, she immediately sweeps Sam into her arms and offers him a cookie, not realizing that he's been gorging on them all afternoon. She always asks about his day, and he usually tells her that he has spent the afternoon watching TV and playing video games.

Recently Sam has become a difficult sleeper. He can't fall asleep and wakes up during the night complaining of nightmares. He has been begging to sleep in the family bed and, too tired to put up a fight, Stacey and Jordan have relented. Now Sam sleeps happily sprawled out between his parents, but Stacey and Jordan complain that they are up all night.

Day 11

Many parents—even parents who are rigid about their own behavior—find it hard to have their children maintain a nutritious diet and get enough exercise. They don't see that along with adequate rest, nutrition and exercise form the foundation of good health. And recent research has suggested that all three basic human needs are related.

A well-balanced diet helps children be alert and active during the day but calm and restful at night, and limiting sugar, caffeine, and food additives is particularly important if your child has trouble going to sleep.

Years ago, most children naturally got enough exercise by running around and playing. Many of today's children, even those as young as three and four, do not get enough exercise. Children spend less time in outdoors active play than ever before and more time in front of the TV and the computer. This change in their activity level has significantly contributed to the obesity epidemic that has become a national crisis.

Do you think that your family has a healthy lifestyle? Do you and your children get enough sleep and have good nutrition and exercise habits? If you are not sure, the following exercise may help.

Becoming the Parent You Want to Be

Keeping a log will give you a true picture of whether your family has good health habits. Make seven copies of the chart below, and fill in one a day for a week. Use a scale of 1 to 5 to rate the nutritional value of each meal, with 1 = poor and 5 = excellent.

	Hours of Sleep	Breakfast	Lunch	Dinner	Hours of Exercise
Mom					
Dad					
Child 1					
Child 2					
Child 3					

It's a Fact

Some 13 percent of six- to eleven-year-olds are considered overweight, and the percentage of overweight children ages two to six is also rising.

Did your child get a Happy Face or other reward for sleeping in his or her own bed?

_____

Write down how your child reacted.

_____

_____

_____

_____

What do you need to change about your family's nutritional habits?

_____

_____

What do you need to change about your family's exercise habits?

_____

_____

What three small steps can you take to begin changing your family's lifestyle?

_____

_____

_____

You're really flying high!

Today you'll learn how your child can be taught to calm himself when he is too wound up or upset to sleep.

Does This Sound Like Your Family?

"I can't fall asleep!" seven-year-old Haley called to her mother, who was comfortably reading in her own bed.

"Just try," her mother called back.

Ten minutes passed, and Haley called again, "I still can't fall asleep."

"Try some more," her mother replied, a little irritation creeping into her voice.

This back-and-forth went on three more times, and then Haley upped the ante. "Can I come sleep next to you?" she said, in a plaintive voice.

"Come on in," her mother said with resignation.

Haley crawled into bed next to her mother. She was asleep in a matter of minutes, and her mother kept reading. Haley was too big for her mother to pick up and move back into her own bed, as she used to do. So mother and daughter slept together, yet again, in the same bed.

Many parents say that their children end up in the family bed because they can't fall asleep. Children might say that they are afraid of a monster in the closet or worried about a test, a recital, or a sick relative. Sometimes they claim that they are just not tired. Of course if you just leave your child alone, she will eventually fall asleep, assuming that the lights stay out. But anxious children may stay up for many hours past their bedtime, and when they have to wake up early to go to school, their actual time asleep can be severely reduced. This lack of sleep reduces their serotonin levels, making them more likely to feel anxious. This cycle can go on for months and even years, unless their parents intervene by teaching them to self-calm.

There are many ways you can teach your children to relax and self-calm, including deep breathing, muscle relaxation, guided imagery, yoga, and listening to calming music. It is not something you want to teach your child at bedtime. Instead, choose a self-calming exercise that suits your child and practice it in the early evening, when your child (and you) can use a transition from the activity of the day to the quiet of the evening.

Many psychologists prescribe relaxation exercises for anxious children or children with anger-control problems, but in truth, this is an activity that can help all children. Self-calming has both mental and physical health benefits; there is some evidence that practicing relaxation techniques on a daily basis contributes to an overall sense of well-being and, by lowering the pulse rate and blood pressure while relaxing the muscles, can help with many chronic diseases.

Self-calming takes just ten minutes a day, and it will not only teach your child a new kind of self-care, but it will help her make that all-important journey into restful sleep.

Day 12

Becoming the Parent You Want to Be

Take ten minutes today to teach your children, four and older, deep breathing (sometimes called belly breathing). When we tell children to breathe deeply, they often puff out their chests and raise their shoulders to their ears, but this actually causes tension in the neck. Instead, you want your child to do abdominal breathing, expanding his tummy so that it rises as he inhales and falls as he exhales.

The first step is to put a sticker on his tummy, and then have him recline on a sofa or a soft chair. To the count of three, have your child take a deep breath and watch his belly as the sticker rises up. Then have him let out his breath out slowly, watching the sticker go down as he does. Repeat the abdominal breathing ten times, and you do it too! Put on soft relaxing music while you both practice deep breathing to clear your minds and soothe the day's cares away.

It's a Fact

Studies tell us that 75-90 percent of visits to a physician's office are for stress-related conditions and complaints. Learning to relax is the number one way to deal with stress.

Did your child get a Happy Face or other reward for sleeping in his or her own bed?

_____

Write down how your child reacted.

_____

_____

_____

_____

How did you sleep last night? _____

Do you think you have more stress than most people? _____

Do you build relaxation time into your day? _____

What can you do to reduce stress for your family?

_____

_____

_____

_____

_____

That was great!

Dealing with Separation Anxiety

Today you'll learn how to deal with children who are anxious when they are away from their parents at night.

Does This Sound Like Your Family?

Meredith was concerned about her daughter Chloe, an adorable two-year-old who was becoming more and more clingy. Chloe did not want to be left alone with her grandparents or even her babysitter, whom she had known from infancy. Even though Meredith worked from home to be near her daughter and was available all day long, Chloe had started to become anxious when her mom stepped out of the room, even insisting on being in the bathroom with her.

Although Chloe had always been content in her crib, she now screamed when she was put into it, holding her little hands out to her mother with a look of sheer terror in her eyes, a look that Meredith could not bear. Invariably Meredith would pick Chloe up and bring her into the family bed, where she would comfortably snuggle next to her mother for the night.

Now it was the look in Meredith's husband's eyes that caught her attention—not a look of terror, but one that clearly said, "When is this going to end?"

Separation anxiety disorder is common at different stages in a child's life, and there are different degrees of severity. Mild separation anxiety is to be expected when children go a new school or stay with a new babysitter or simply go through a challenging phase of development. Some children have intense and prolonged anxiety when away from their parents. If your child is being left with a familiar caregiver and extreme anxiety persists even after four weeks, consider it a red flag.

Becoming the Parent You Want to Be

Check off the behaviors that describe your child. A child who engages in more than five of these behaviors during a period of four weeks may be suffering from a separation anxiety disorder that can be helped with professional guidance.

☐ Displaying excessive distress during separation from a parent or loved one

☐ Exhibiting panic on separation or in anticipation of separation

☐ Expressing fear of loss (death, separation, change)

☐ Expressing fear of being kidnapped or lost

☐ Exhibiting physical symptoms during separation

☐ Following parents around at home and expressing fear of being alone or even in a separate room

☐ Preferring to spend time with a parent rather than friends

☐ Having nightmares about separation

☐ Experiencing anxiety about loved ones getting sick or going away

☐ Panicking if a parent or caregiver is late and needing reassurance that they will arrive

☐ Expressing fear of attending field trips, sleepovers, and birthday parties

☐ Displaying excessive neediness or connection, for example, by frequently saying "I love you"

☐ Reacting to disapproval with a high level of stress

Most likely, you will have checked off no more than two of the behaviors listed earlier. While many children have separation issues, particularly at night, it is not usually a true disorder and can generally be alleviated with some simple techniques. Here are some I recommend:

- Select a special stuffed animal to be your child's nighttime friend. Have the stuffed animal sleep next to you for three or four nights. Then give it to your child, saying something like: "This bedtime bear has been sleeping with me to get all of my good smells and good love. Now he will sleep with you in your own bed, and you can snuggle with him all night long."

- When your child first gets into bed, use the deep breathing introduced on Day 12 to help him calm down.

- Use guided imagery tapes to help distract and calm your child. There are several commercial CDs available in stores and on the Internet.

Review what you learned this week about developing a consistent bedtime ritual and teaching your child about the importance of sleep. Focus on the positive steps you can take to help your child deal with bedtime anxiety.

It's a Fact

Anxiety disorders are caused by an overactive amygdala, a small almond-shaped structure in the brain that regulates emotions. Studies show that early training can calm an overactive amygdala, making children significantly less prone to developing serious anxiety disorders.

Did your child get a Happy Face or other reward for sleeping in his or her own bed?

_____

Write down how your child reacted.

_____

_____

_____

_____

How did you sleep last night? _____

Would you say that you are an anxious person? _____

How about your spouse? _____

Is there anything you are doing that may contribute to your child's separation anxiety?

_____

_____

_____

_____

I think you're great!

Today you'll learn how to help your child deal with nightmares.

Does This Sound Like Your Family?

Josh's new job meant that he came home after Shana had already put three-year-old Max to bed. Max had been used to his father's being there for dinner, and the change made him anxious.

About two weeks after Josh's job started, Max began having nightmares about a monster coming through his bedroom window and kidnapping him. He would wake up crying and rush to his parents' room, where he'd crawl into the bed next to Josh. This went on for a week, until Josh finally took Max back to his own bedroom and sat down on the bed, trying to calm him and explain that the monsters were just in his imagination, not real. But Max couldn't calm down, and the nightmares continued.

Josh was already tired from his new job, and his son's fidgety sleeping often woke him up throughout the night. Although his job was a promotion, and they certainly needed the extra income, Josh wondered whether the change was really worth it. Since Max had started having nightmares, nothing had been the same in their house.

Nightmares are a frequent cause of children's sleeping with their parents. This is not a problem if it happens once in a while, but it can lead to a pattern of cosleeping that disrupts the parents' sleep and gives children the message that they can't deal with their fears by themselves.

Almost all children experience nightmares occasionally. They can begin as early as two but are most common among children three to six years old. No one really knows why nightmares evolved, but they seem to be related to normal everyday anxieties. They can happen in cycles; a child may have bad dreams over a period of a few weeks, which may stop for months and then recur.

For the most part, you shouldn't be concerned about nightmares even when they are frequent. Some slight alterations in your child's sleep habits will usually help. Look at this list of dos and don'ts, and see if any of these can help you and your child through a period of nightmares.

Do

- Monitor television viewing and eliminate scary or violent programs, particularly those close to bedtime.
- Go in when she first wakes up with a nightmare. Waiting until she is wide-awake and overwrought will usually make it harder for her to go back to sleep.
- Stay with your child for as long as it takes her to calm down. Reading a book or telling a story will likely take her mind off the nightmare.
- Explain in a calm, reassuring voice that it's safe to go back to sleep.
- Support your child by remaining calm. If you also show anxiety, it will make her anxiety much worse.
- Talk about the content of the nightmare if your child is old enough to verbalize it. You can show her ways to make up happy endings and confront dangers. If she doesn't feel like talking, don't force her.

Don't

- Wake up your child. If you hear her cry out but she's still asleep when you get to the room, wait to see if she really wakes up. Children can often go right back to sleep without even knowing you're there.
- Tell your child it was just a dream. To your child, the nightmare was very, very real. You may want to explain that you have dreams too and that you go right back to sleep if a dream wakes you up.
- Talk about the nightmare immediately after it has occurred. This may only increase your child's anxiety. If your child wants to talk about it, wait until the morning.

Day 14

Becoming the Parent You Want to Be

There are many different techniques you can use to help children with nightmares, and one of my favorites borrows from a Native American tradition.

Based on the belief that the night air is filled with dreams, both good and bad, the tradition involves hanging a dream catcher that swings freely in the air and catches the dreams as they flow by. Dream catchers are hoops with string or yarn loosely woven in various patterns and are typically decorated with beads and feathers. The good dreams pass through the weaving and gently slide down the soft feathers. The bad dreams get tangled in the dream catcher and perish with the first light of the new day.

You can buy dream catchers on dozens of sites on the Internet, some simple and some painstakingly crafted by Native Americans. You can also create your own dream catcher; there are simple instructions to make dream catchers for and with kids at www.dream-catchers.org.

After you buy or make your dream catcher, explain to your child the magic of how it will work. Hang it near your child's bed, so that she can look at it just before she goes to sleep. If a nightmare wakes her, check the dream catcher and say something like, "Look at this! Most of your nightmare got caught right in your dream catcher, but a little must have gotten through, and it woke you up. Let's shine a light at your dream catcher and get rid of it." Then take a flashlight and shine it at the dream catcher. The next morning, you can say something like: "Your dream catcher is letting too many nightmares through. Let's get some string and make the holes a little smaller so that no nightmares get through."

Nightmares are perfectly normal, and all children have them periodically. If your child's nightmares persist and are accompanied by physical symptoms or other daytime anxieties, you may want to visit the pediatrician to make sure that all is well.

It's a Fact

What a child dreams about is influenced by three factors: his emotional and physical development; the emotional conflicts he is dealing with; and his daytime events and experiences.

Did your child get a Happy Face or other reward for sleeping in his or her own bed?

_____

Write down how your child reacted.

_____

_____

_____

_____

How did you sleep last night? _____

Did you have nightmares as a child? _____

What is the worst nightmare you can remember?

_____

_____

_____

_____

Are there situations that may be contributing to your child's nightmares?

_____

_____

_____

You're a winner!

Week 3:
Raising Self-Reliant Kids

By choosing to get your child out of the family bed, you are taking an important step in helping her become an independent, well-adjusted adult. As an infant, your child was totally dependent on you to fulfill all her needs, but at as early as two years of age, children enter a different phase, where their developmental wiring tells them to go forth and become unique people. This is an age when children love to do things themselves, insisting that they can put on their own jackets, tie their own shoes, and make their own decisions. As a parent your job is to provide encouragement for their newfound sense of autonomy and independence while gently reminding them of their limits and being ready to lend a helping hand.

Cosleeping goes against your child's need to be autonomous. Keeping your child in your bed or bedroom past the age of two gives her the message that she is still dependent on you to make the transition from the activity of the day to the peaceful calm of the night.

This week you will learn many ways to help your child become a self-reliant and resilient person. You will learn how to help him deal with frustration, be more responsible, have a positive attitude, and also know when to respect authority and be more compliant. All of these new emotional and behavioral skills will help your child make the transition from sleeping with you to sleeping by himself. They will also build the foundation for your child to cope with other kinds of life transitions. The activities you will learn in this section can be used well after the 21-day program ends.

Day 15

Teaching Your Child to Deal with Frustration

Today you'll think about how to help your child become more patient and better able to handle disappointment.

Does This Sound Like Your Family?

Marilyn and Dave are in their midforties. After ten long years of trying to get pregnant, they decided to adopt a child, and Owen, now three and a half, is the center of their universe.

When Owen first came into their home as a fourteen-month-old, he was a quiet and watchful toddler, but with the adoring attention of his parents, he soon became as rambunctious as any of Marilyn and Dave's twelve nieces and nephews. Owen's parents loved his spirited and outgoing personality, but they were not sure how to handle the increasing evidence that he had a real problem coping with frustration.

When Owen was building with his wooden blocks and unexpectedly knocked some down, he would howl and beat his hands against the floor. Sometimes he would throw the blocks across the room. When he turned on the TV and his favorite show wasn't on, he would pout and flip through the channels with the remote. When he sat down to eat and his food wasn't ready, he would pound the table with his fists until his mother or father would stick a piece of bread or a cracker in his mouth, just to keep him quiet.

Owen's need to have everything his own way had become a problem at his preschool, too. He had to be first in line; he didn't want to share toys; and if he wasn't tired, he refused to take a nap even though all the other children were.

Owen insisted on sleeping in his parents' bed every night. Sometimes he would fall asleep on the couch, and then his father would put him in his own bed, but when he woke up, he would scream for his parents. Not surprisingly, Owen always got his way when it came to bedtime battles.

Marilyn and Dave hoped their son was just going through a phase, like the terrible twos or the fearsome fours. They didn't want to think about what the future had in store if this was a permanent part of Owen's personality.

Some children have an easy disposition and don't ever seem to have a problem being patient. Other children, like Owen, seem to become more strong-willed with every passing day and are increasingly vocal when they don't get their way. Most children fall between these extremes, being patient sometimes and impatient others, depending on their mood, the time of day, or whether they had a good night's rest.

But we live in a culture that rarely rewards patience or the ability to tolerate frustration. We want everything as fast as we can get it: fast cash from the ATM, fast meals from the microwave, fast Internet connections. Advances in technology have made life easier and easier, and when it is difficult, we are often unprepared to cope.

In a famous experiment, a group of four-year-olds were individually taken to a room with a one-way mirror and told to sit quietly while the researcher did an errand. The researcher then put a marshmallow in front of the child and said, "If you don't eat this marshmallow, I'll give you a second marshmallow when I come back." As you might guess, many of the children couldn't resist the frustration and immediately ate the treat. Some were so upset by the challenge that they burst into tears. Others sat quietly until the researcher came back, and then got the reward for waiting patiently.

These same four-year-olds were followed for the next twelve years. Most were completing high school when the researchers gave them tests to assess qualities like self-esteem, and also evaluated their success in school. The children who didn't eat the marshmallows, who showed self-control and frustration tolerance as four-year-olds, did significantly better in school and in general had a higher degree of self-acceptance than the other children. Surprisingly they did better on their grades and even on standardized tests than their brighter peers who had less self-control.

Day 15

Becoming the Parent You Want to Be

Several activities presented earlier in this book have already helped you teach your child to be patient and to tolerate frustration, including the activities in the first week that showed you how to become less permissive and develop more appropriate ways to deal with misbehavior.

In under ten minutes, the Tough-Task Triathlon provides a more direct approach to helping children, ages four and up, learn how to handle frustration. It deliberately frustrates your child on three separate tasks, and he will win points depending on how well he can tolerate the frustration. You make the important difference in his success by encouraging his effort, even when the task is very difficult.

The Tough-Task Triathlon

Before You Play

You'll need a watch or stopwatch, a spoon, a small ball (about the size of a golf ball), a deck of cards, and coins.

How to Play

For each task, deduct a point each time your child shows any sign of frustration, such as complaining or making a face. Give him plenty of praise for dealing calmly with frustration.

- Begin by asking the child to balance the ball on the spoon and walk across the room. Your child gets one point for each step taken without dropping the ball.
- In the second task, ask your child to build a house of cards. Time him for three minutes. He gets one point for each card standing in the card house.
- In the third task, ask him to spin coins on a smooth tabletop. Time him for three minutes. The player gets one point for each coin that spins for at least a count of five.
- If, at the end of three rounds, he has accumulated seven points or more, declare him a winner. If he does not have seven points, he can play again.

It's a Fact

If you teach your child to deal with frustration, he will be much less likely to argue or test your limits when it is time to sleep in his own bed. And children who learn to be more patient with problems and to tolerate frustration invariably become more cooperative and do better at school.

Did your child get a Happy Face or other reward for sleeping in his or her own bed?

_____

Write down how your child reacted.

_____

_____

_____

_____

How did you sleep last night? _____

How did your child do on the frustration tasks? _____

How would you say that you and your spouse are at handling frustration?

_____

What are some other ways you can teach your children the importance of being patient?

_____

_____

_____

_____

_____

You are awesome!

Today you'll learn how to teach your child to be more responsible for his behavior.

Does This Sound Like Your Family?

Petra was a healthy and capable seven-year-old. She was a gymnast and captain of her soccer team. She was an eager and bright student and well liked by her teacher. Yet an observer watching Petra interact with her mother might think that she had some physical problems or learning problems, or that she was much younger than seven.

Petra's mother dressed her every morning and bathed her every night, just as she had done all her life. She made all Petra's playdates and kept track of her homework and school assignments. At meals, she waited on Petra like she was visiting royalty, running to get anything Petra needed, buttering her bread, and cutting her meat.

Occasionally Petra would say, "I can do that myself," and Petra's mother would typically respond, "Oh, I don't mind." Yet if Petra left her schoolbooks on the bus or forgot to feed her pet hamster, her mother would irritably say, "Why aren't you more responsible?" Petra would shrug her shoulders and wait a moment until her mother's anger passed. Then things would continue just as before.

Many parents foster dependency in their children by doing too much for them. They pick up their children's clothes and put away their toys. They stand over their children when they brush their teeth or wash their faces, instead of letting them do these tasks without supervision. Not surprisingly, these parents don't require children to help out around the house. Children can learn to do simple chores like putting socks in a drawer or toys in a toy chest as early as two years of age, but many go through their elementary school and even teen years without a single household responsibility.

When parents don't teach children to be responsible, they are usually content to remain dependent. Of course they will eventually decide that some things are private and none of their parents' business, and they will do these things for themselves, but they will not learn that being a responsible person is an important part of being in a family, a friendship, or a community.

Cosleeping also fosters dependency in children, and it does not teach them to be responsible for going to bed on time, waking up on time, and getting a good night's rest. When you make being responsible an important value in your home, it will be much easier for your child to understand why he must sleep in his own bed.

Raising responsible and self-reliant children can be hard work, but it is well worth the effort. Responsible children—just like a responsible spouse or coworker—will help you with both small and large tasks so that you don't feel like you are shouldering all of life's burdens by yourself. Here are some tips to help you raise responsible children:

- **Make responsibility a priority in your home.** Think twice before you do things for your child who is over three. Ask yourself, "Is this something my child could do for himself?"

- **Give your child age-appropriate tasks and chores.** Young children enjoy doing household tasks, like helping to fold laundry or wiping off a table. Take advantage of this early interest in helping you out! By five, children should have regular chores that they do every day, and every year they should do a little more. (See suggested chores for different ages in Appendix C.)

- **Be a good role model; do tasks on time and without undue complaint.** If you put off washing the dishes or complain about making your bed, your child will do the same.

Day 16

- **Don't rescue your child.** Some parents are quick to jump in when their children complain about the difficulty of their homework or household tasks. Encourage your child to do these things without your help. You can give guidance and support, of course, but don't do your child's work just because it is hard.

- **Teach your child about cause and effect.** What happens if your child does not put away his toys? What happens if he forgets to bring his lunch to school? Talk to your child about the consequences of his actions as well as his inactions, and let him experience firsthand the result of being irresponsible.

- **Have high expectations.** Some parents say that they want to let their kids be kids rather than saddling them with lots of responsibility. While this may sound like a reasonable idea, studies tell us that children are happier when their parents expect them to be responsible. Generally speaking, families that expect a lot of their kids raise children with a higher degree of self-worth.

Becoming the Parent You Want to Be

Contracts are a great way to help kids learn to be responsible. The contract on the next page can be filled in with any number of tasks or expectations that you have of your child, such as:

- "I will only watch TV for a half hour a day."
- "I will do my chores and homework on time."
- "I will follow safety rules while on my bike."
- "I will only use the Internet when my parents are in the room."

Make sure that you and your child sign the contract. Give your child plenty of praise and attention whenever you see responsible behavior.

Day 16

My Responsibility Contract

I _____ promise that I will
   (name of child)

_____.

(task or expectation)

I will do this on time and correctly without the need for reminders.

Signed

_____

Child

_____

Parent

It's a Fact

Money management is part of teaching kids responsibility. As soon as kids can count (at age three to five), they can begin to earn a small allowance of a quarter or fifty cents. I usually recommend that first graders receive a dollar a week, second graders receive two dollars a week, and so on.

Did your child get a Happy Face or other reward for sleeping in his or her own bed?

_____

Write down how your child reacted.

_____

_____

_____

_____

How did you sleep last night? _____

Can you think of other ways to make your child more responsible?

_____

_____

_____

Do you think that you "rescue" your child from responsibilities by doing them yourself? Give an example.

_____

_____

_____

_____

_____

You deserve a hug!

Today you'll learn the importance of encouraging a positive attitude in your child, and how this will make your life together much easier.

Does This Sound Like Your Family?

"Angie is not an easy child," her mother explained to Angie's first-grade teacher. "She always sees the negative in things, rather than the positive. If it's sunny, she'll say, 'I bet it's going to rain tomorrow.' If she makes a new friend, she says that the girl is 'just okay' but she'd rather be friends with someone else. She is always so negative that it's hard for her to be happy. I'm worried that this attitude will affect her schoolwork, too."

Angie's mother's worries are well founded. Children with negative attitudes do have more difficulties than children with positive attitudes, in their families, with their friends, and with their studies. Research done at the University of Pennsylvania has consistently shown that optimism—seeing the positive aspects of a situation and believing that negative things can be changed for the better—helps children cope with both small and large problems. Optimistic children are not only happier than other children of the same age, but they tend to perform better in school and are at lower risk for depression and other mental health problems.

Some children, like Angie, seem to be born pessimists, while others seem to be born optimists. The good news is that even if your child was born with a more negative attitude, you can teach her how to be more positive. If you do, everyone will reap the benefits.

Becoming the Parent You Want to Be

If you want your children to have a positive attitude, research tells us exactly where you have to begin—by assessing your own attitude. Children learn their thinking style from their parents, so if you or your spouse are negative and pessimistic thinkers, it is most likely that your child will be the same way. If you want him to have a positive attitude, you will have to show him how. So watch what you say in front of your child!

There are many activities that can help you teach your child the importance of a positive attitude. One of my favorite is called a Positive Feelings Family Scavenger Hunt. In this simple game, players have ten minutes to gather five things that make them feel good. Then players bring these objects to the living room and share why they make them feel good.

This simple game focuses your child on finding what is positive in his life, and it does the same thing for you. It also gives you the opportunity to show your child the kinds of things that make you happy, so you can also use this little game to teach important values.

It's a Fact

You will find many great activities that encourage optimism and positive thinking at www. fishfulthinking.com. This website (sponsored by Goldfish crackers, which accounts for its name) is dedicated to making positive thinking a part of every family's day and has activities for parents, kids, and teachers.

Did your child get a Happy Face or other reward for sleeping in his or her own bed?

_____

Write down how your child reacted.

_____

_____

_____

_____

How did you sleep last night? _____

Give an example of a time when having a positive attitude helped you cope.

_____

_____

Who is the most positive and optimistic person you know? How does this attitude help that person?

_____

_____

_____

Who is the most negative person you know? How does this attitude hurt that person?

_____

_____

_____

You are so special!

Communicating Better with Your Child

Today you'll learn better ways to communicate with your child so that you can understand each other's needs.

Does This Sound Like Your Family?

At the end of the day, Valerie was as exhausted as a person could be. She and her parents owned a small restaurant in an upscale suburb, and the work hours seemed endless. As a self-taught cook, Valerie loved using fresh ingredients in unusual combinations, but that required lots of extra time going to the organic market and experimenting with new recipes.

Valerie had five-year-old Dawn dropped off at the restaurant after preschool, and Dawn would play with her stuffed animals or watch TV in the kitchen or sometimes help out washing the vegetables. Dawn seemed to enjoy the hustle and bustle of the kitchen, yet Valerie had noticed in the last few weeks that her daughter was getting quieter and quieter and seemed to be sad about something.

"What's wrong, honey?" Valerie asked her daughter, as they both munched on homemade cookies during a break from the kitchen duties.

"Nothing," Dawn replied.

"Are you sure?" Valerie asked. "You look like something is wrong."

"Nothing is wrong," Dawn said again, and she kept her gaze on the plate of cookies.

"Well, you know you can tell me if anything is wrong," Valerie said. "You can tell me anything at all."

"Okay," Dawn said, but Valerie thought there was little conviction in her daughter's voice. She thought she might call the teacher the next day and see if she could give her any insight.

Day 18

Most parents ask their children about their day as soon as they get home, and most parents get a similar reply.

"What did you do today?"

"Nothing."

"Did anything special happen?"

"Nope."

"Anything good?"

"Nah."

"Anything bad?"

"Nah."

Of course some children are more chatty than others, and they may talk in detail about the activities of the day, particularly about the social gossip, but even these children may become quiet when something is bothering them. When it comes to getting your child to leave the family bed or for any difficult transition, open communication will certainly help. You and your child will feel better when you can discuss your feelings, even if they are difficult feelings and even if you disagree.

Psychologists have long understood the value, and the difficulty, in getting children to open up about their feelings. Most psychologists have a variety of techniques that they use to help children begin to talk about their feelings, but few are so easy and successful as the use of art. It doesn't seem to matter what medium you choose; art can help kids talk about their feelings, while direct questioning only seems to close them up.

Here are some art techniques that can help get your child talking when she is going through a difficult time, or just any time at all. The more often your family talks about feelings, the easier your days—and nights—will be.

- **Family drawings:** Sit down with your child in front of a large piece of paper. With pencils and crayons, just draw together and talk about whatever comes to mind.

- **The scribble technique:** Ask your child to scribble a line. Then ask him to make that scribble into a picture, and have him make up a story about the picture.

- **Colorful feelings:** Tell your child that colors represent different feelings, and ask him to pick eight colors to represent eight feelings (for example, red means angry, blue means sad, and so on). Ask your child to draw a picture, using color to represent the feelings it portrays.

- **Draw a wish:** Ask your child to draw something she is wishing for.

- **Pounding out feelings:** Give your child a lump of clay and ask him to pound it flat while talking about all the things that make him mad.

- **Draw a dream:** Ask your child to draw a dream that she would like to have. She can put the drawing under her pillow and try to have that dream. (Some parents find that this is a good technique to help kids with nightmares.)

- **The feelings X-ray machine:** Use the drawing in the next section to help kids draw the different feelings they have inside.

Becoming the Parent You Want to Be

The Feelings X-Ray Machine can be used anytime to help kids express the feelings inside them. Just make a copy of the drawing on the next page, and give your child a box of crayons to color his feelings.

It's a Fact

When children talk about their feelings, their brains produce a biochemical called serotonin, one of the most important brain chemicals that helps balance their mood. There are many other ways to stimulate the production of serotonin, including exercise, being out in the sun, and eating a balanced diet.

Did your child get a Happy Face or other reward for sleeping in his or her own bed?

_____

Write down how your child reacted.

_____

_____

_____

_____

How did you sleep last night? _____

Do you think that your discipline style affects your ability to get your child out of the family bed?

_____

Do you have a problem being firm and consistent? _____

If the answer is yes, who can help you with your approach to discipline?

_____

_____

_____

_____

You're a shining star!

Day 19

Teaching Your Child to Solve Her Own Problems

> Today you'll learn how to help your child solve her own problems. Children who can solve problems effectively are better at coping with the anxiety that may prevent them from sleeping on their own.

Does This Sound Like Your Family?

"What should I do, Dad?" was the question seven-year-old Neil asked his father nearly every day. On Monday, Neil was upset because he had been picked last for the softball team. On Tuesday, Neil left his math workbook in school. On Wednesday, he thought his friend Reid was mad at him. And so it went for the rest of the week, as Neil fretted about his daily predicaments.

Most of the time his father tried to get Neil to solve his own problems, saying, "What do you think you should do?" But Neil would just reply, "I don't know. That's why I'm asking," and then his father would give him advice. Neil would usually take this advice, but sometimes he begged his father to take whatever action was required: talking to the softball coach, driving to the school to get Neil's homework, or calling Reid's parents to see if there was a problem.

Neil's parents were facing a problem of their own: Neil's fretting was interfering with his sleep and he would often climb into their bed. After several nights of interrupted sleep, his father ruefully said to his mother, "Let's ask ourselves the question I always ask Neil: what do we think we should do?"

Some children seem to worry more than others, and this can be hard for parents to witness. In extreme cases, children may be diagnosed with anxiety disorders, but many children who worry are just not skilled at problem solving. Children are capable of solving all kinds of interpersonal problems at as early as four years of age, but they often don't realize they have this ability until they are much older. And being logical and analytic in academic subjects doesn't necessarily translate into being a good problem solver when it comes to personal problems. Psychologists believe that problem solving that involves emotions originates in a different part of the brain than the reasoning and rational thinking that children use to solve math problems.

Many parents are overprotective of their young children and continue to anticipate problems and shield children from discomfort as their children grow older. You can help your child meet the inevitable challenges of growing by teaching him to be a good problem solver when it comes to his emotional life. Instead of feeling that you have to have all the answers, you can encourage your child to find his own solutions when he is upset. For example, if your child protests about sleeping in his own bed, you might say something like: "I know that this is not something that you want, but I'm afraid you can't always have what you want. What are some ways that you can make this situation better?"

Becoming the Parent You Want to Be

Helping your child become a better problem solver is not simply a matter of asking her to work out her own difficulties; you have to teach most children the steps to becoming a good problem solver. If your child is at least five and has difficulty in solving her problems, the following activity might help. Solutions Tic-Tac-Toe is a five-minute game based on a program called I Can Problem Solve, developed at Hahneman University by Myrna Shur and David Spivak.

Solutions Tic-Tac-Toe

Before You Play

Using index cards, make a deck of twenty or more "problem" cards by writing down real-life problems your child is facing. Your child can help you think about these problems.

How to Play

- Shuffle the cards.
- Your child goes first, selecting the top card and reading the problem aloud.
- Play a traditional game of Tic-Tac-Toe, but write down an "X" or an "O" only when you suggest a realistic possible solution to the chosen problem.
- If a player cannot suggest a good solution, he loses his turn.
- Write down all the solutions generated for each round of Tic-Tac-Toe.

After you have played this game several times, try using it to solve this problem: How can we make it easier for you to sleep every night in your own bed? You may be surprised at the solutions that your child comes up with.

Of course, if you think your child's inability to solve problems is due to excessive anxiety, consider having him evaluated by a psychologist. There are many good programs that can help children with anxiety disorders, and these techniques are always most successful when children are young. (You may also want to look at another book in the Instant Help Workbook series, *I Bet I Won't Fret*, by Dr. Timothy Sisemore.)

It's a Fact

Research attests to the fact that children as young as four years of age can be taught how to solve interpersonal problems. Teaching children how to problem solve is effective in helping them with behavior problems, including anger management, and often has the added effect of improving their schoolwork.

Did your child get a Happy Face or other reward for sleeping in his or her own bed?

_____

Write down how your child reacted.

_____

_____

_____

_____

How did you sleep last night? _____

How did you and your child do on the solutions game? _____

Is anxiety a problem in your life or in your spouse's life? _____

Were you shy or anxious as a child? Can you think of an example?

_____

_____

_____

How did you deal with anxiety when you were young? Could these coping strategies help your child?

_____

_____

_____

You're a great kid!

Day 20

Teaching Your Child to Do What He Is Asked

> Today you'll learn how to get your child to do what you want without an argument or backtalk.

Does This Sound Like Your Family?

"I don't want to," Hannah said, standing with her hands on her hips.

"Too bad," replied her mother. "I want you to brush your teeth and get into bed, and I'm the parent."

"But I'm still playing," Hannah told her mother, "and I'm the child."

"It's not the same thing," Hannah's mom said. "Parents make the rules, and children follow them."

"Well, children should make the rules," Hannah said adamantly. "They're not dummies, are they?"

"I didn't say children are dummies," Hannah's mom said quickly. "Children aren't dummies, but they aren't grown-ups either. And grown-ups make the rules."

"Who said grown-ups make the rules?" was Hannah's reply.

More than parents in many other cultures, Americans tend to reward their children for independent and creative thinking, and even for questioning authority. But questioning authority can sometimes lead to being willful and disrespectful to adults, and this is never a good thing.

Do you feel that your child listens to your requests and respectfully follows them? I am assuming that your answer is no, or you wouldn't be reading this book. If your child were more compliant, you would simply say, "I want you to sleep in your own bed," and that would be the end of it.

Children who question authority often do so in many areas of family life. Do you frequently find yourself asking your child again and again to do something? Do you find that you have to raise your voice and even get angry to get your child's attention? Do you find yourself threatening your child when she doesn't follow your requests? If you have answered yes to any of these questions, the following activity might help.

Becoming the Parent You Want to Be

When parents have difficulty getting their children to follow their requests, there is one mistake I find they are making over and over again: they talk too much.

I often tell parents that it is great to talk to their kids throughout the day, but not when they are trying to get the kids to do something they don't want to do, like starting their homework, doing their chores, or getting ready to sleep in their own beds. At these times, the less talk the better. Too many parents I know negotiate with their kids, giving their children the message that rules are not really meant to be followed.

Stop negotiating! Just make your requests in a calm but firm tone, and then don't say anything else. In fact, you don't even have to say anything at all. I developed the Good Behavior Road Signs on the following pages for parents to just hold up as reminders of what they want their children to do. There are seven preprinted signs and an eighth for you to fill in with your own directive. To prepare the signs just do the following:

- Make copies and cut them out.
- Mount them on a piece of cardboard.
- Tape a flat craft stick (like a large popsicle stick) on the back of each sign.
- Now hold up the appropriate sign when you want your child to do something. And remember to praise your child for doing what you ask.

It's a Fact

Nonverbal communication is much more powerful than words alone. Studies tell us that words account for only 10 percent of our communication with others, while visual messages account for nearly 60 percent of how we communicate.

A Parent's Guide to Getting Kids Out of the Family Bed

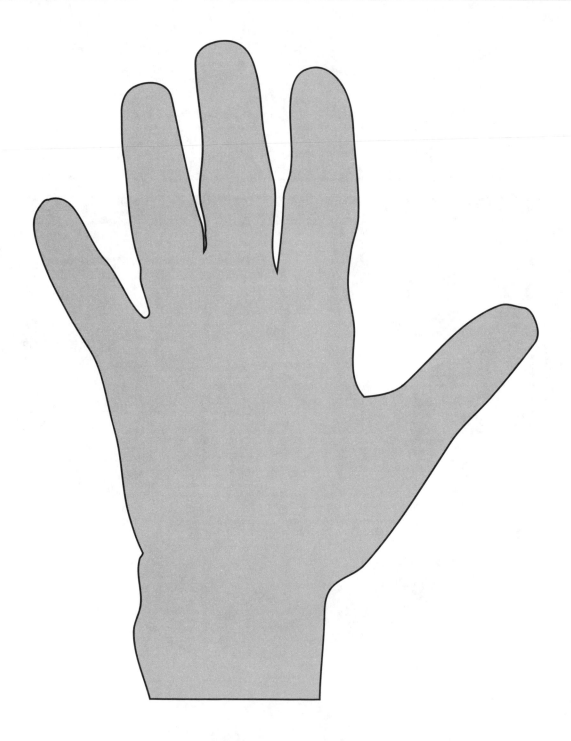

A Parent's Guide to Getting Kids Out of the Family Bed

A Parent's Guide to Getting Kids Out of the Family Bed

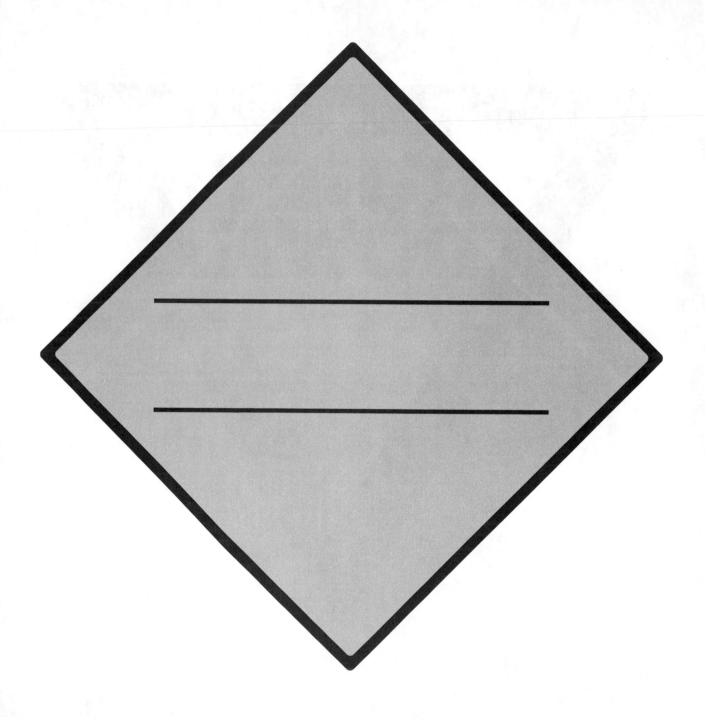

Did your child get a Happy Face or other reward for sleeping in his or her own bed?

_____

Write down how your child reacted.

_____

_____

_____

_____

How did you sleep last night? _____

Do you feel that your child listens to your requests and respects them?

_____

Do you need to expect more of your child? _____

Did the road signs help your child do what you asked without an argument? If so, what did you learn about your child from this activity?

_____

_____

_____

_____

_____

You are super!

Time to Lighten Up Day 21

> Today you'll learn the importance of connecting with your family through humor and play, no matter what difficulties or struggles the week may bring.

Does This Sound Like Your Family?

It had been a typical week for Anna and Jake and their three children. Jake commuted an hour and half to his job in the city. Anna worked part-time and spent a good deal of time driving her three active children around. It was Friday night, and the family was just beginning dinner at eight o'clock, because their father's train had been late. They all sat in silence, except for three-year-old Matty, who always had something to say.

"Can you tune her down?" Craig, age twelve, asked his parents. "I've got a headache."

"Yeah," said six-year-old Catherine, "can't we get some quiet around here?"

In a weary voice, Anna said, "Matty, can you be quiet at the dinner table, and then you and I can play some games after dinner?"

"Why?" Matty asked. "Why can't I talk when I want to?"

"Because you never stop talking," Craig answered for his mother, "and it's time for some quiet."

Matty thought about this for a minute, then asked, "Why should we be quiet? Why can't we have some fun?"

"Because..." Jake started and then stopped. "Why should we be quiet at dinner?" he thought to himself. "Isn't family time supposed to be fun?"

Day 21

While it's true that parenting is not all fun and games, many parents find that their time as a family is the most stressful part of their day, and a surprising number of adults say that they find work more relaxing and fun than their time at home. That isn't good.

No one has to tell children the benefits of humor and play; it is a part of their natural way of being in the world. But if you aren't making fun a priority in your life, here are some reminders of why it is so important:

- Laughter lowers your blood pressure.
- Laughter improves your immune system.
- Laughter provides a way to bring you closer to other people.
- Laughter lightens your mood.
- Laughter lowers your stress hormones.
- Laughter makes you happy to be alive!

If you have been following this 21-day program as suggested, you have spent many hours thinking about your children and the various transitions they will go through, including the transition to sleeping in their own beds. But today is the time to end the program on the right note, by having fun with your kids. Why is humor and play and laughter important in this program? Because you are giving up some degree of closeness with your children in getting them out of the family bed. Having fun with them, every single day, will bring that closeness right back in a much more appropriate way.

Becoming the Parent You Want to Be

On a scale from 1 to 10, how much fun do you have with your family? Use 1 for "Not much at all," and 10 for "Every day is a blast." Be honest with your answer.

If your answer is under 5, it's time for a family fun make-over. Using humor and play to connect with your child is easy to do. Here are some ideas to bring more fun into your home.

- Play the Laugh Out Loud Game once a week. This game lasts just fifteen minutes, and the rules are simple: Everyone has to laugh before the game ends. Family members can tell jokes, make faces, tickle each other, or do anything they think will be funny.

- Create a Humor Center. Designate a place in the home, like a bulletin board or the refrigerator, where family members can post cartoons, jokes, funny messages, and so on.

- Play a favorite sport, but have everyone play with their opposite hand.

- Watch a funny TV show or video together.

- Take a trip to the zoo and watch the monkeys. Then when you get home, imitate what they do.

- Go through a photo album and look at funny pictures.

Write your own ideas here:

_____

_____

_____

_____

_____

Day 21

Write your spouse's ideas here:

_____

_____

_____

_____

Write your child's ideas here:

_____

_____

_____

_____

It's a Fact

Children with good senses of humor tend to be more social and have a higher sense of self-worth, and they are typically better liked by their peers.

Did your child get a Happy Face or other reward for sleeping in his or her own bed?

_____

Write down how your child reacted.

_____

_____

_____

_____

How did you sleep last night? _____

Describe a really fun time you had with your family.

_____

_____

_____

Can you do something every day that will make family life more fun? Write it on your calendar.

_____

Is there something keeping you from having more fun with your family? What can you do about this?

_____

_____

_____

You are my #1!

Epilogue

Congratulations on completing this 21-day program! You have no doubt learned a lot about yourself as well as your child, and you have taken an important step in shaping the emotional development of your child.

No matter what your child's age, you can continue helping him with his emotional, behavioral, and social development. As you have learned, the first step is providing your child with a clear structure defined by household rules that are consistently enforced.

If you have another behavioral issue to address, you can adapt the program and give your child a Happy Face or a certificate for each day he performs the behavior you want to encourage. Perhaps you are wondering why I chose 21 days. This is the average time it takes to form a new positive habit that will become easy to repeat. For example, if your child is working on a behavior like doing his homework on time, and he does it for 21 days without any reminders, he is likely to keep doing his homework on time, but if you try a behavioral program for fewer than 21 days, or are inconsistent in using it, your child will be more likely to slip back into old habits. Of course even after the 21 days are up, you child still needs reinforcement, so remember to give your child plenty of praise and affection when he behaves in positive ways.

In completing this program, you have also learned some new ways to communicate with your child. You have used games, art activities, and stories to help teach your child new emotional and behavioral skills. By all means, keep this up! Many parents don't realize that they can play an important part in shaping their child's emotional development by spending just ten to fifteen minutes a day doing simple and fun activities. You may want to review some of the other workbooks in our Instant Help series; they can help you help your child with a variety of common problems, including shyness, adjusting to divorce, and dealing with loss, among others. Visit our website at www.InstantHelpBooks.com.

Appendix A:
21-Day Happy-Face Chart

Child's name: _____

Date you began: _____

Appendix B:
Do You Have a Strong-Willed Child?

Strong-willed children need consistent rules and consistent discipline, but they also need more help in learning empathy, cooperation, and helpfulness. If you check any three of these statements, then you likely have a strong-willed child. You can learn more about the best ways to help your child either by reading or by consulting a counselor.

- ☐ My child always wants to have his way.
- ☐ My child is quick to anger.
- ☐ My child doesn't like to take turns.
- ☐ My child doesn't like to share.
- ☐ My child frequently talks back to me or other adults.
- ☐ My child gets upset when her schedule changes.
- ☐ My child is always trying to test the limits.
- ☐ My child has difficulty making friends.
- ☐ My child frequently gets into trouble at school.
- ☐ My child refuses to go out on errands with me.

Appendix C:
Age-Appropriate Chores

Two- to four-year-olds can:

- Put away toys
- Carry silverware, napkins, and so on to the table
- Empty wastebaskets
- Sort clothes

Five- to six-year-olds can:

- Make beds
- Dust furniture
- Feed family pets
- Hang up clothes
- Rake the yard
- Sweep

Seven- to eight-year-olds can:

- Set and clear the table
- Water plants
- Vacuum
- Wash dishes

Nine- to ten-year-olds can:

- Make and pack their lunch
- Fold laundry
- Help with yard work
- Load and unload the dishwasher

Eleven- to twelve-year-olds can:

- Do laundry (with supervision)
- Walk pets
- Clean the bathroom or kitchen
- Wash the car

Lawrence E. Shapiro, PhD, is a nationally recognized child psychologist who is known for his innovative, play-oriented techniques. He has written over two dozen books and created over forty therapeutic games. Shapiro is founder of the Childswork/Childsplay catalog and publishing company, a leading distributor of psychologically oriented toys and games. He is author of numerous books, including *How to Raise a Child with a High EQ: A Parent's Guide to Emotional Intelligence* and *The Secret Language of Children*.

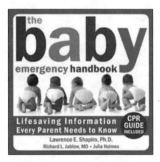